The
Oral Tradition
in the South

The
⋯⋙❲ Oral Tradition ❳⋘⋯
in the South

WALDO W. BRADEN

Louisiana State University Press
BATON ROUGE AND LONDON

Designer: Joanna Hill
Typeface: Linotron 202 Garamond #3
Typesetter: G & S Typesetters, Inc.
Printer: Thomson-Shore
Binder: John Dekker & Sons

Library of Congress Cataloging in Publication Data

Braden, Waldo Warder, 1911–
   The oral tradition in the South.
   Bibliography: p.
   Includes index.
   1. Oratory—Southern States—Addresses, essays,
lectures.   II. Title.
PN4055.U52S682   1983   808.5'1'0975   82-20827
ISBN 0-8071-1093-0

For my students

Contents

Preface

In *The Mind of the South*, W. J. Cash wrote that "rhetoric . . . early became a passion—and not only a passion but a primary standard of judgment, the *sine qua non* of leadership" in the antebellum South. He could have added that this passion grew out of an oral tradition that pervaded southern living from the cabin to the statehouse and found expression in storytelling, courtroom pleading, revival preaching, and, of course, in electioneering. The South was truly an oral society. Being more attuned to the spoken word than to the printed page, southerners looked upon their speakers as important sources of information, inspiration, and entertainment, and regarded them along with warriors and hunters as heroes. Eager listeners gathered from miles around to participate in festivities, revivals, and rallies and to listen to their oratorical champions. To them eloquence was the beau ideal of the southern way of life.

The phrase "southern oratory" has become stereotyped and has been associated with widely diverse speakers who flourished anywhere in the vast South from the time of Patrick Henry to the present. Through the years the elusive label has taken on various connotations. When referring to speeches of the Old South, it suggested eloquence and high purpose. After the Civil War, it characterized the ornate, grandiloquent, and myth-laden ceremonial oratory that had become the vogue. In the twentieth century it has often been applied in a derogatory sense, especially when used to designate the speeches of the so-called demagogues. Further complicating its several connotations, users of the term have obscured it in legend and myth. Some observers have gone so far as to declare "southern oratory" to be a genre all its own.

The present six essays attempt to ventilate this fascinating, myth-encrusted phrase, setting forth some distinctions among the various groups of speakers. The goal is to place southern public address in a meaningful context, to provide insight into its dimensions and complexities, and hence to get a little closer to the flesh-and-blood speakers who attracted great followings in the South.

The essays fall into a rough chronological sequence. The first, entitled "The Emergence of the Concept of Southern Oratory, 1850–1950," stands apart from the other five and traces the evolution of the concept through the entire period, taking note of the mythmaking process in school readers, literary histories, anthologies, and historical works. An earlier form of this essay, one of the first I wrote on the subject, became a preface for my other writing and the background for several graduate studies that I directed. It prepares the ground for the other five essays.

The next two essays, "The Oral Tradition in the Old South" and "The 1860 Election Campaign in Western Tennessee," reflect on antebellum speaking. The first of the pair discusses the pervasiveness of an oral tradition that nurtured rhetorical activities. The second, a case study of a brief moment in the intense campaign of 1860, is included to suggest some of the flavor of what went into antebellum political canvasses.

The fourth essay, "Myths in a Rhetorical Context," is a companion piece to "Repining over an Irrevocable Past: The Ceremonial Orator in a Defeated Society, 1865–1900," an essay published in my *Oratory in the New South*. These two essays consider how the postwar ceremonial speakers, who worked to restore the self-esteem of defeated Confederates, gave vigor to the great myths of the Old South, the Lost Cause, the Solid South, and the New South. The essay herein discusses how the myth works in rhetorical discourse. Although the concept of myth has a wider implication in other rhetorical studies, here it throws light on why the speakers who employed the southern myths entranced the natives. The essay "Repining over an Irrevocable Past" extends this discussion and applies myth analysis to the postwar speakers.

The so-called southern demagogues of the twentieth century changed southern speaking in that they departed from the grandiloquence and expansive manner of nineteenth-century southerners. Although they did not overlook the persuasive power of the great myths, they found other rhetorical means to reach the common folk, emphasizing their own similarities to, and identifying with, their poor constituents. In contrast to the patriarchs of the past, they sought the rural touch and spoke in the common idiom, at times becoming clowns, showmen, and "medicine men." They found their forte in exploiting the sensitivities, weaknesses, and yearnings of poor rural southerners who had been previously ignored and denied effective representation. Bold and crass, they won followings through fomenting class conflict and hatred.

In the final two essays I explore what I have termed a "rhetoric of exploitation." The first generalizes about the demagogues as a group. The final one, a case study of a closed society, shows how persuaders, desperate for power, minimized outside influences and gained control by substituting fear, compulsion, coercion, and discipline for voluntary acceptance.

Some of these six essays have appeared in other forms for other occasions. With one exception they were first given as lectures at colleges and universities. Four of them were presented as the Forty-seventh Annual Distinguished Lectures in Speech at Louisiana State University, September 10–16, 1981, and were repeated in a similar series jointly sponsored by Carson-Newman College and the University of Tennessee, March 29–April 2, 1982. Three of the essays were published in an earlier form in the *Southern Speech Communication*

Journal. Two essays appear in the present volume for the first time in print. I have consciously avoided repeating here what appeared in the two volumes on southern oratory that I edited. The present collection, plus those two volumes, are intended to constitute a corpus of criticism on southern oratory from 1830 to 1970.

Acknowledgments

In a sense this book has been under way for about twenty-five years. During these years I have received help and counsel from many persons, too many to name at this time. Nevertheless, I am well aware that I could not have made it without their support.

Pleasantly I recall how my students and I pursued the study of southern public address together. They provided inspiration and insights, and asked me searching questions when I was attempting to clarify my thinking. Likewise, I am indebted to those who heard much of this material in public lectures at conventions and university gatherings. The several journal editors through whose hands many of the chapters passed encouraged me to refine my writing and saved me from some embarrassing slips. I have also profited greatly from the careful and enlightening criticism of Ralph T. Eubanks of the University of West Florida. He has been a good friend. Likewise, Harold D. Mixon of Louisiana State University has checked out many of my interpretations. Our conversations over coffee have been most helpful.

The Department of Speech of Louisiana State University and the Louisiana State University Press have provided me with an encouraging atmosphere. Of course the editors of the Press, always highly competent, have helped me considerably and have given freely of their time. I am much indebted to my secretaries: Myra Fitts, Jean Jackson, and Sue Beauclair. I wish to thank the Southern Speech

Communication Association for permission to reprint the following articles: "The Emergence of the Concept of Southern Oratory," *Southern Speech Journal*, XXVI (1961), 123–83; "Myths in a Rhetorical Context," *Southern Speech Communication Journal*, XL (1975), 113–26; and "The Rhetoric of a Closed Society," *Southern Speech Communication Journal*, XLV (1980), 333–51. I also wish to thank Harper and Row for permission to reprint "The Campaign for Memphis," from *Antislavery and Disunion*, ed. J. Jeffery Auer (New York, 1963), 225–41.

The
Oral Tradition
in the South

The Emergence of the Concept
of Southern Oratory, 1850–1950

In the little book *Myths and Men*, Bernard Mayo discusses the popular images of Patrick Henry, George Washington, and Thomas Jefferson and concludes that "they have been so long uncritically praised, and dispraised, that all three are heavily myth-encrusted. Each presents a formidable challenge to the historian-detective who would separate the flesh-and-blood man from the obscuring legend."[1] It is equally evident that the phrase "southern oratory" is likewise "heavily myth-encrusted"; it is also clear that the rhetorical critic and historian are challenged to separate the flesh-and-blood oratory, to adapt a phrase from Mayo, from "the obscuring legend."

When and where did this popular image have its start? This question is difficult to answer. On September 5, 1840, the *Maine Cultivator*, an agricultural paper in Hallowell, observed that "stump oratory" is a "Southern fashion."[2] In June, 1844, in the *Democratic Monthly Magazine*, a writer declared that a Virginia speaker differed from a New Englander in that he was "less complicated, with less apparent paradoxes, hospitable, generous, liberal and even profuse in his indulgences. . . . There is a certain moral grandeur in his mind suited to great conceptions. . . . As a speaker he is apt to be florid in his style." Frederick L. Olmsted, writing in 1856, suggested that "Southern

1. Bernard Mayo, *Myths and Men* (Athens, Ga., 1959), 2.
2. This phrase was called to my attention by Robert G. Gunderson, who quoted it in his book *The Log Cabin Campaign* (Lexington, Ky., 1957), 162.

legal oratory" was characterized by the "excessive use of metaphors and figures of speech, and of rodomontade."[3] These three bits of evidence from widely scattered sources suggest that the popular image was held by some writers before the Civil War. A more diligent search would probably uncover many similar examples dating back even earlier.

The mythmaker may tell you that he identifies a "southern orator" by "how he sounds," making him a mellifluous fellow who uses grandiloquent language, a rich dramatic voice, and an impassioned delivery. The genre of southern oratory was said to be "self conscious, sometimes almost histrionic, stately and excessively dignified, fervidly eloquent, sometimes surcharged with fervid aspiration or denunciation, heavily weighed with tandem substantives and marshalled epithets, and with carefully balanced phrase and clause." The stereotype is suggested in a description of William L. Yancey: "Unlike the preacher described by Lincoln, who looked as if he were fighting bees, Yancey stood perfectly still. He made none of the theatrical gestures which were the stock in trade in most Southern orators." Historian Clement Eaton said of the delegates to the Nashville Convention of 1850 that they "were inspired . . . to unfurl their most elegant figures of speech, their most graceful gestures, and their richest tones of forensic eloquence." Charles W. Kent, literary editor of *The Library of Southern Literature*, characterized the antebellum orator as one who spoke "with a freedom approaching volubility and a love of ornamentation tempting to indulgence in high coloring."[4]

3. Quoted by Robert C. Jeffrey, "Men, Movements and Materials for Research in Public Address in Virginia," *Southern Speech Journal*, XXIV (1959), 154; Frederick Law Olmsted, *A Journey in the Seaboard Slave States* (New York, 1856), 638.

4. George Armstrong Wauchope (comp.), *The Writers of South Carolina* (Columbia, 1910), 42; Arnold Whitridge, *No Compromise* (New York, 1960), 63; Clement Eaton, *Freedom of Thought in the Old South* (Durham, N.C., 1940), 50–51; Charles W. Kent, "Southern Literature: A Brief Sketch," in *The Library of Southern Literature*, ed. Edwin Anderson Alderman and Joel Chandler Harris (15 vols.; Atlanta, 1907–13), XI, 5038.

A brighter image made southern oratory synonymous with eloquence. In this vein the mythmaker presents the speaker as being superior to competitors from other sections in perception, creativeness, language, and delivery. At times this twist is no more than a variation of the floridity theme; but there is usually a difference that supports southern pride and is more satisfying to the apologist, for it does not demean heroes and martyrs. About 1900 C. Alphonso Smith, an English professor, was telling audiences, "In all that constitutes true eloquence, in that subtle union of manly thought with impassioned utterance, the South can challenge comparison with any nation and with any age." The novelist Joseph Hergesheimer, who indulged in mythmaking in a book called *Swords and Roses*, dressed up the image as follows: "The most dignified profession of the deep South before secession was statesmanship. . . . It was almost wholly founded on the power of oratory, the music and magic of a voice." Again, Montrose Moses, a literary historian, thought that orators were "creative artists—speaking with almost a prophetic touch of inspiration that rises above close analysis, and plays upon feeling." He continued: "The full length portrait . . . is one of tremendous color, of solid fame . . . nobility of pose. Upon his face are marked the firm lines of command, of conviction, of set purpose; within his eyes shine beneficence, kindliness, intelligence, deep sentiment, humor. His pose is stately, and is a measure of his solid stand in life." Clearly the cloak suggested by Moses was big enough to fit almost any hero, whether he was statesman, general, or orator.[5]

In its beginnings the phrase southern oratory must have emerged when southerners began comparing themselves to Yankees and wishing that they could claim greater cultural and intellectual attainments. Even in colonial times, southerners set themselves apart from their northern neighbors. Historians confirm that a real southern

5. C. Alphonso Smith, *Southern Literary Studies: A Collection of Literary, Biographical and Other Sketches* (Chapel Hill, 1927), 85; Joseph Hergesheimer, *Swords and Roses* (New York, 1929), 35; Montrose J. Moses, *The Literature of the South* (New York, 1910), 209, 217.

nationalism commenced to develop after 1820, first in Virginia and South Carolina and later in all plantation areas. By 1850 southerners, seeing themselves as Cavaliers, took pride in their aristocratic leanings and found satisfaction in contrasting themselves with "penny-pinching" Yankees. The phrase southern oratory is closely kin to a whole indigenous clan of images: southern way of life, southern hospitality, southern womanhood, southern literature, southern writers, and southern thought. These romantic phrases, widely used and accepted, probably won status when the natives wanted to assert their superiority over the Yankees. T. Harry Williams has noted that the southerner has a "great ability to deceive himself as well as to spoof the outsiders. . . . Far beyond any native competitors, he is marvelously adept at creating mind-pictures of his world or of the larger world around him—images that he wants to believe, that are real to him and that he will insist others accept."[6]

And so it is generally with such myths, images, or symbols that are uttered so frequently and so loosely: their very illusiveness increases their popularity, charm, and respectability. Phantomlike, they are difficult to locate at a place and in time, and difficult to define or even describe. But to track them down, determine their dimensions, and analyze their sources becomes a first step in driving away the ghosts and in getting a little closer to the flesh-and-blood people who really lived.

The ensuing investigation, which turned into a project in rhetorical sleuthing, involved a study of school readers, literary histories, anthologies of speeches, and historical works. My search uncovered five interesting school readers: *The Southern Reader and Speaker* (Charleston: William R. Babcock; Richmond: Drinker and Morris; Mobile: J. K. Randall), published in 1848; Jonathan J. Judge's *The Southern*

6. Carl N. Degler, *Place over Time: The Continuity of Southern Distinctiveness* (Baton Rouge, 1977), 27–65; Rollin G. Osterweis, *Romanticism and Nationalism in the Old South* (Baton Rouge, 1967); T. Harry Williams, *Romance and Realism in Southern Politics* (Athens, Ga., 1961), 7.

Orator (Montgomery: Brittan and De Wolfe), published in 1853; D. Barton Ross's *The Southern Speaker* (New Orleans: J. B. Steel), published in 1856; Richard Sterling's *Southern Orator* (New York: Owen and Agar; Greensboro, N.C.: R. Sterling and Sons), published in 1856; and Sterling's *Little Southern Orator* (Macon, Ga.: J. W. Burke), published in 1872. These books are collections of one- and two-page excerpts from orations, poems, and dialogues. They are comparable to readers such as *The United States Speaker*, the *National Orator*, the *Columbian Orator*, and "some scores of District school readers, courses of readings, etc. emanating from New England."[7] The impetus for these textbooks grew out of the irritation that southerners felt at having their sons memorize and recite selections denouncing "abstract evils of slavery." Ross dedicated his *Southern Speaker* "to the Student who is receiving his education among the endeared associations of his own beautiful 'sunny South' away from the annoyances of fanaticism."

School readers, particularly those by McGuffey, contributed much to the training of future orators. What the beginner memorized and recited he later imitated and attempted to match. Eaton claims that the McGuffey readers were designed "to inculcate morality, patriotism and devotion to orthodox religion" and that they "inspired young boys to become orators."[8] Of course, the memorization and imitation of speech models have been favorite means of developing eloquence since the time of ancient Greece. This line of thought raises the question of what influence these five readers and others like them had on those who later became southern orators. At best an answer can only be speculative.

First, of course, these books certainly accentuated the desirability of striving for eloquence, setting high goals for their students. Reciting the thoughts of men like Daniel Webster, Henry Clay, and John C. Calhoun encouraged students to take as heroes men who had

7. *De Bow's Review*, XXI (1856), 650–51.
8. Clement Eaton, *A History of the Old South* (Durham, N.C., 1940), 478.

excelled with the spoken word. Likewise, the novices became aware that public address had played important roles in historic events—the American Revolution, the founding of the new nation, the great compromises, the great debates on the nature of the Union, and the forensic efforts of the leading lawyers. As each youth took his turn upon the platform before his peers, admiring parents, and approving teachers, he perhaps experienced for the first time the excitement of facing listeners and commenced to dream of speaking to grander audiences on great occasions. And many did.

Second, these readers, true to their motivation, fostered admiration of the South—its heroes and its institutions. To promote southern pride these collections included many excerpts from southern writers and speakers, making heroes of such figures and omitting what was critical of the region and its people. The books led the student to read, memorize, and declaim eulogies. Judge devoted fourteen selections to this form of speaking; Ross, thirty-five; Sterling, thirty-nine. Washington was a favorite of the three, as was the great triumvirate of Clay, Calhoun, and Webster. Surprisingly, the New Englander received more attention than either of the southerners. Lafayette was also greatly admired. Ross included orators' eulogies of S. S. Prentiss and H. W. Hilliard, while Sterling saw fit to print addresses eulogizing Andrew Butler and Hugh White. In a long list of suggested titles for written composition, Sterling included only one Civil War general—Stonewall Jackson. But he also suggested as good subjects George Washington, Thomas Jefferson, Patrick Henry, Andrew Johnson, John C. Calhoun, Daniel Webster, and Henry Clay.

Ross and Sterling devoted a surprising amount of space to Daniel Webster. In addition to twenty selections from Webster, Ross provided two eulogies of New England's favorite son—one by H. W. Hilliard and a second by John M. Clayton. It is doubtful whether schoolboys could resist admiring Webster when they recited: "Our country has produced some great men. They glow in the heaven of the past like stars in the firmament and in that splendid constellation we see Webster in full-orbed glory." Ironically, if the fledglings developed into so-called southern orators by imitation, they may have learned much from the famous New Englander at the same time. This admiration of Webster was not incongruous with the spirit of slavocracy, because Webster, as a man of both property and political power, probably had more in common with wealthy southern Whigs than he did with many northerners. What he said about the Constitution and the Union did not frighten or alienate many southerners, who admired his courageous stand in 1850.

Third, the compilers of these readers, like many of their contemporaries, markedly preferred the polished, grand, and ornate style. For instance, they excerpted passages from eulogy perorations, choosing the very sections likely to be emotional and figurative, or what has been called "extravagant and studded with over-statement . . . hortatory and evangelistic."[9] In truth, the students who read and memorized selections from these books were attuned to the high-flown style associated with southern oratory. Through imitation they probably reechoed these tendencies and rhythms in their later speaking and writing.

Fourth, contrary to what one might anticipate, the content of these readers was conservatively American. They contained comparatively little that could be considered overly sentimental about the South. One possible explanation is that these books were published before the postwar fad of indulging in nostalgia for the genteel living of the Old South. At a later period, no doubt, such readers probably would have given much more attention to war heroes and to popular southern myths. But in these books the young orator was encouraged to devote his loyalties to the Constitution and the Union.

The stereotype of the southern orator previously cited did not gain widespread acceptance until the first decade of the twentieth century. Prior to 1900 there appeared no anthology of southern speeches and

9. William G. Carleton, "The Celebrity Cult a Century Ago," *Georgia Review,* XIV (1960), 133–42.

not a single title on southern oratory in *Poole's Index to Periodical Literature*. Then suddenly, within a ten-year period, an outburst of interest in the subject produced several books. It was of course a part of an intellectual awakening that swept through southern institutions of higher learning. The post-Reconstruction generation, "children of a cultural famine that blighted the land of their youth," was replaced by young, vigorous personalities who received their training at Johns Hopkins and Columbia and commenced to infiltrate southern campuses, particularly those in North Carolina, Virginia, and Louisiana. The appearance of these young men represented a shift away from the "broken-down clergyman-professor to the trained specialist." Motivated by interest in their region, these new scholars sought to determine what deserved to endure and what was genuinely "southern." Often cited as typical of the group were W. L. Fleming, Edwin Mims, William P. Trent, and C. Alphonso Smith.[10]

To C. Alphonso Smith, a professor of English, falls the distinction of being one of the first to present the stereotyped southern orator in a full-blown form. On February 5, 1895, he gave a speech entitled "Southern Oratory Before the War" to the state legislature of Louisiana. During the next twenty-five years he repeated this lecture at commencements and student assemblies across the South.[11]

---

10. C. Vann Woodward, *Origins of the New South, 1877–1913* (Baton Rouge, 1951), 429, 440–46.

11. There is a manuscript of the speech in the C. Alphonso Smith Papers, University of Virginia Library, Charlottesville. Smith delivered the speech again at the Millsaps College commencement, Jackson, Mississippi, June 7, 1897. In his papers he listed eleven other instances, dating from 1903 to 1922, when he returned to this topic: April 13, 1903, College of Charleston, Charleston, South Carolina; December 31, 1907, Gastonia, North Carolina; February 4, 1913, Cabell Hall, University of Virginia; February 8, 1913, Jefferson Society, University of Virginia; March 28, 1913, high school, Richmond, Virginia; January 12, 1915, Washington and Lee University, Lexington, Virginia; February 15, 1917, Winchester, Virginia; May 5, 1917, Jefferson Hall, University of Virginia; July 15, 1920, high school, Asheville, North Carolina; June 20, 1921, agricultural and engineering college, Raleigh, North Carolina; June 14, 1922, University of South Carolina, Columbia, South Carolina; June 30, 1922, Winthrop College, Rock Hill, South Carolina.

Smith pursued hortatory goals, not critical or scholarly ones. Seeking to stir southern pride, he said the orators constituted "the most interesting, instructive and inspiring chapters in American history . . . yet to be written." He also hoped to refute the notion of the cultural insignificance of the South and urged careful study of the genre of southern oratory, because, he said, "the influence of the great orators . . . has never . . . received adequate recognition," and "the great orations of the past [are] a heritage, sacred and priceless." Calling the roll of those whom he considered among the foremost southern speakers, Smith cited Patrick Henry, John C. Calhoun, Henry Clay, John Randolph, Robert Y. Hayne, Seargent S. Prentiss, Benjamin Hill, Alexander Stephens, Robert Toombs, Judah P. Benjamin, Jefferson Davis, and L. Q. C. Lamar. As he moved from campus to campus, he must have stimulated or heightened interest in, and discussion of, the topic among other professors of literature and history. It is not surprising that ideas that Smith developed were consistent with what later appeared in the literary histories and anthologies. Whether these thoughts were the common property of these authors and anthologists, who had all come under the same cultural influences, or whether one of them stood above the others, is difficult to untangle. It is true that professors at the University of North Carolina and the University of Virginia, both of which were schools where Smith taught, took the lead in urging the study of southern speakers. But Smith expressed his ideas on the subject long before any of the authors and anthologists of these volumes joined either of these faculties, and as a ceremonial speaker he was more active than any of the others in popularizing the subject.[12]

At this distance, seeing Smith in perspective and determining his influence is difficult. But a good guess is possible. The sources that he consulted reflected on American, not southern, speaking; none of them suggested, described, or even mentioned the stereotype of the

12. For a more complete analysis, see Waldo W. Braden, "C. Alphonso Smith on 'Southern Oratory Before the War,'" *Southern Speech Journal*, XXXVI (1970), 127–38.

southern orator. The responsibility for developing and emotionalizing the image clearly seems to belong to Smith, nurtured in the post-Confederate years when mythmaking and hero worship were popular. Although he denied a desire "to stir again the embers" of social controversy, Smith made heroes of these southern orators and endowed them with great virtues and superior ability. Aware of prevailing southern attitudes, he returned to his subject repeatedly, for he found welcome listeners, sensitive about their cultural and intellectual standing in the nation.

Because of his reputation as a scholar, his popularity as a speaker, and his status as a professor (over the years he taught at three of the leading southern universities), he lent credence to the growing myth. What he said probably encouraged other writers to promote the myth instead of a flesh-and-blood representation of the typical speaker of the South.

It is my impression that the southern literary historians helped foster the growing image of southern oratory. Hard pressed to collect a sufficient body of "southern literature," they naturally turned to what was abundantly available—oratorical pieces. Moved by the same forces that stirred Smith, they too were eager to put the South's culture on a footing with other sections; consequently, the first literary histories and collections of southern writings took note of the subject of southern oratory. In 1905, William P. Trent, who taught first at the University of the South and later at Columbia University, brought out *Southern Writers*, an anthology that he said was designed primarily for use in schools and colleges of the South and for supplementary readings and information in classes of American literature, history, composition, and rhetoric. He suggested that his goal was to include material showing that southerners had contributed "a larger and a better share to the literature of the Republic than is generally admitted." Within the scope of what he recognized as literature, he included the contributions of the "statesmen and orators." "Publicists and orators were," he explained, "of course, produced in abundance,

Calhoun easily taking the lead as a subtle expounder of the right of minorities. The fame of these old-time speakers—Hayne, Toombs, Stephens, Yancey, Seargent S. Prentiss . . . is still fresh, but rather through tradition than through much reading of such of their speeches as are in print." For his anthology Trent chose excerpts from speeches by eleven orators: 1) George Washington's Farewell Address, 1796; 2) Patrick Henry's speech climaxing with the famous words "Give me liberty or give me death," 1775; 3) Thomas Jefferson's first inaugural address, 1801; 4) the speech by John Randolph of Roanoke on the Greek question, delivered in the House, January 24, 1824; 5) Robert Y. Hayne's debate with Webster, 1830; 6) John C. Calhoun's speech on the slave question, March 4, 1850; 7) Robert E. Lee's speech of acceptance of the command of the Army of Northern Virginia, 1862; 8) Jefferson Davis' Senate speech on the transcontinental railway, January, 1859, and his farewell speech to the Senate, January 21, 1861; 9) Alexander Stephens' "A Plea for the Union," delivered at Milledgeville, Georgia, November 14, 1860; 10) L. Q. C. Lamar's eulogy of Sumner, 1874; and 11) Henry W. Grady's "The New South," 1886.[13]

A year after the appearance of the Trent volume, Carl Holliday (1879–1936), who at the time taught at the Alabama State Normal and later at the University of Virginia, published *History of Southern Literature*. The preface declared that his goal was to call attention to "that body of literature—much of it worthy indeed of permanency—which has arisen in the South." In a chapter entitled "The Period of Expansion (1810–1850)," he included a consideration of "orators, essayists, and historians." He lent his hand to mythmaking, saying, "The country courthouse resounded not infrequently with bombastic harangues, but more often with eloquence of a very high order. Every cross-road had its debating club. . . . It was but natural that the

---

13. W. P. Trent (ed.), *Southern Writers: Selections in Prose and Verse* (New York, 1905). For a similar text prepared for high school students, see Edwin Mims and Bruce R. Payne (eds.), *Southern Prose and Poetry* (New York, 1910). The latter book includes a section entitled "Orations and Address" (357–421).

Southern statesman of the day should, through his power of publicly expressing thought, gain the admiration of all Americans." Holliday also discussed the oratorical careers of John Randolph, Henry Clay, John C. Calhoun, Thomas Hart Benton, and Robert Y. Hayne. In his characterization of Calhoun and Hayne, he illustrated how the myth of southern oratory continued to thrive. Finding Calhoun's simplicity and logic difficult to explain in terms of his conception of southern speaking, Holliday admitted that the South Carolinian could "use beautiful illustrations"; but he thought Calhoun failed to show "a rich imagination" or the "ability to surprise by a flash" on the printed page. To Holliday "the epitome of extremely Southern characteristics" was the "fiery eloquence" of Robert Y. Hayne. "His speeches often swept along with a rush that did not always permit his listeners to pause for thought, but instead, carried them away as willing captives. So filled with passion were his words that at times he seemed almost beside himself, and yet for a moment lost control of the flood of words." [14] In Holliday's view "eloquence of a very high order" was emotional rather than intellectual, provided vivid pictures, apt comparisons, and forcible illustrations, showed rich imagination and an ability to surprise by a flash, was fluent, vigorous, fiery and passionate. To illustrate his discussion, he quoted flowery paragraphs and cited brief eulogistic tributes from biographers.

In a book called *The Writers of South Carolina*, George Armstrong Wauchope (1862–1943), professor of English at the University of South Carolina, echoing the sentiments of the other writers, described the "old fashioned rhetorical style" of his state's speakers as "highly decorative and artificial." [15] He too selected his material from epideictic, mostly eulogistic oratory.

In *The Literature of the South*, a literary history that has been characterized as "the best general study" of its kind, Montrose J. Moses included one chapter entitled "Voices of the Old South: Being a Consideration of the Literary Claims of the Orators—Typified in Calhoun, Clay, and Hayne." In another chapter, called "Social

14. Carl Holliday, *History of Southern Literature* (New York, 1906), 123–40.
15. Wauchope (comp.), *The Writers of South Carolina*, 142.

Forces," he discussed "the orators of secession"—Yancey, Toombs, and Stephens. Writing with greater perspective and less apology than most southern commentators of the day, Moses analyzed the southern speaker in a larger historical setting and observed that southern writers and orators "developed [their rhetoric] in a plethora of high sounding phrases, colored by excess of feeling, without any particular reference to proposition." Although he granted that the southern orators were sincere and courageous, he charged that they failed in originality of thinking and that their style was "ponderous," "laid on," "high sounding and excessive in emotion and feeling." Moses thus represented an early attempt to see southern rhetoric in its true light.[16]

The three collections of southern oratory that appeared between 1908 and 1910 gave impetus to the concentrated study of southern oratory but in no way challenged the growing image of the southern orator. Edwin Dubois Shurter, professor of oratory at the University of Texas, included in his *Oratory of the South* eighty-four speech excerpts, of which seventy-three were from ceremonial speeches delivered after the Civil War. The following year a two-volume set, *Eloquent Sons of the South: A Handbook of Southern Oratory*, embraced as "representative examples" sixteen of "the most widely known statesmen and publicists of the South." A third anthology, entitled *Southern Orators, Speeches and Orations*, designed for the secondary schools and edited by Joseph Moore McConnell, professor of history at Davidson College, recognized thirty-four orators in its 350 pages.[17]

The most significant development in southern scholarship during the following decade was the publication of two ambitious multivolume

16. Robert E. Spiller *et al.*, *Literary History of the United States* (3 vols.; New York, 1948), III, 308; Montrose J. Moses, *The Literature of the South* (New York, 1910).

17. Edwin Dubois Shurter, *Oratory of the South* (New York, 1908); John Temple Graves, Clark Howell, and Walter Williams (eds.), *Eloquent Sons of the South: A Handbook of Southern Oratory* (2 vols.; Boston, 1908); Joseph Moore McConnell, *Southern Orators, Speeches and Orations* (New York, 1910). The latter book probably grew out of a dissertation, "Southern Oratory from 1829 to 1860," completed in

works on the South's history and literature. There can be little doubt that the editors of *The Library of Southern Literature*, a sixteen-volume set, gave impetus to the study of southern oratory.[18] Led by Edwin A. Alderman, longtime president of the University of Virginia, the principal editors included Joel Chandler Harris, the Atlanta editor, of Uncle Remus fame; Charles W. Kent, professor of English at the University of Virginia; C. Alphonso Smith, professor of English at several southern universities, including North Carolina and Virginia, and prominent lecturer on oratory and literature; and Franklin L. Riley, professor of history at the University of Mississippi and one of the editors of the *World's Orators*.

They enlisted the help of 31 educators, 15 lawyers, 6 clergymen, and 7 newspaper editors and writers. It was truly a massive effort by some of the most talented men of the South. In the finished work they included 68 speakers and quoted portions of more than 100 speeches. (*In toto*, the 16 volumes treated 310 authors and contained about 1,900 selections, including poems, short stories, character sketches, speeches, letters, and essays.) This work demonstrated for the first time the breadth of the subject, mentioning many lesser politicians and several preachers, such as John A. Broadus, Alexander Campbell, and Benjamin Morgan Palmer. The editors included among "fifty reading courses" one entitled "The Orators," made up of 26 lessons "designated for special use of literary clubs and classes in the systematic study." But these editors did not disturb the image of the past. In an essay entitled "Southern Literature," Kent observed that orators of the Old South were "sure of applause of their admiring audiences [and] were not afraid that learning would seem pedantry and oratorical fire mere physical heat."[19] In their selections the editors again showed preferences for ceremonial orations and eloquent bits.

1907 at the University of Virginia in the English department under the direction of Charles W. Kent. This dissertation is now reported lost.

18. My understanding of the set was enhanced by Edith Kay Kirkpatrick, "The Contribution of *The Library of Southern Literature* to the Concept of Southern Oratory" (M.A. thesis, Louisiana State University, 1970).

19. Kent, "Southern Literature," 5038–39.

Nevertheless, they included 40 samples of deliberative speaking, many of which had been delivered in the United States Congress.

By present scholarly standards, the critical essays and some of the selected material show lack of refinement and insight, and certainly more recent investigations and anthologies have surpassed them. But the editors had ambitious goals and a good plan, and are to be commended for coordinating the efforts of so many persons. This work, for the first time, critically surveyed and recognized southern rhetoric and oratory as aspects of the cultural and intellectual life of the region. It pointed to the magnitude of a subject long neglected and ridiculed.

The first full-length single book to attempt an exhaustive treatment of southern public address, and the only one for many years, was Volume IX of a venture in "organized cooperative history" called *The South in the Building of the Nation*.[20] The thirteen-volume collection included discussions of southern history, literature, life, and biography. Thomas E. Watson was assigned the task of editing the volume on public address. He was, of course, a writer and editor, but he was better known as a firebrand orator and Populist politician. Having few qualifications to assemble such materials except his practical experience on the stump, Watson fortunately enlisted the help of five well-qualified contributors: editor Clark Howell of the Atlanta *Constitution*, English professors Edward K. Graham of the University of North Carolina and Benjamin F. Riley of the University of Georgia, attorney John C. Reed, and finally, William V. Byars, who had written *Handbook of Oratory* and had served as principal editor of the *World's Best Orators*. Unfortunately, Watson gave little editorial guidance to his distinguished colleagues.

With the evangelistic fervor of an apologist, Watson sets as his editorial purposes "to recognize and commemorate the work done by public speakers of the South in the creation of popular opinion and

---

20. J. A. C. Chandler *et al.* (eds.), *The South in the Building of the Nation* (13 vols.; Richmond, 1909–13). I gained a better understanding of the Watson volume through Gale K. Byrd, "The Contribution of *The History of Southern Oratory* to the Concept of Southern Oratory" (M.A. thesis, Louisiana State University, 1977).

direction of nationally important events" and "to select some of the more notable characters of southern history and to reveal in their own utterances the manner of men they were." The book is presented in two parts: "History of Oratory" and "Orations and Speeches." The first, encompassing nine chapters (three by Watson), discusses political speaking, the bench and bar, the pulpit, and "general oratory." These chapters have no coherent or consistent plan of development; they overlap and are either little more than running accounts of historical events or catalogs of names with little identification and almost nothing about the orators' actual speaking.

The anthology presents thirty-two items from twenty-eight speakers—twenty-two excerpts and ten complete speeches. How Watson chose his entries is puzzling, for some major figures are represented by brief excerpts from minor efforts, whereas several little-known persons are represented by complete addresses. For example, Watson includes from John C. Calhoun, the South's most distinguished statesman, four paragraphs from a speech on the Oregon question (March 16, 1846) and a portion of a speech on treasury notes (September 19, 1837) but nothing from the debates with Webster on the nature and preservation of the Union. From the long career of Kentuckian Henry Clay, Watson takes only two passages from the introduction and conclusion of a speech on the Seminole War (January 18, 1819).

Having included twenty-eight speakers, Watson overweighted his selection by taking speeches from eight Kentuckians in contrast to only four South Carolinians (though many more were available) and five Georgians, including himself. Among the Kentuckians were four obscure persons: attorneys Ben Lee Hardin (b. 1844), Wilbur E. Browder (b. 1848), and Thomas Francis Marshall (1801–1864), and a Baptist preacher, Edgar U. Mullins (1860–1928).[21] It is to Wat-

21. On the South Carolinians who might have been chosen, see Waldo W. Braden (ed.), *Oratory in the Old South, 1828–1860* (Baton Rouge, 1970), 19–103. The orations of these four Kentuckians were drawn from Bennett Henderson Young (ed.), *Kentucky Eloquence, Past and Present* (Louisville, 1907).

son's credit, however, that he attempted to balance his selections among the various types of speaking, with half coming from legislative speaking.

What were the contributions of these two sets of books to the developing image and the understanding of the genre? Most important, they began to establish the dimensions of the subject, suggesting its diversity and scope by bringing together for the first time excerpts and complete speeches dating from the colonial period to the twentieth century. However, the editors' efforts were insufficient to find many speakers not discussed by the leading historians; their selections were often haphazard and nonrepresentative, tending toward ornate passages and florid ceremonial speeches, both of which confirmed the developing stereotype. The biographical sketches, often abstracted from existing published biographies, included only the best-known events of the orators' lives and accounts of their most important speeches, with no critical evaluation. They provided little information about the orators' speech training and skills.

The Watson volume represents the first extensive attempt at a history of southern public address. Unfortunately, among the nine essays, only the two by Edward K. Graham give a fair picture of important speakers in context. The other seven present little more than running accounts of political happenings or catalogs of names. Many speakers were included because of popular reputation rather than actual speaking abilities.

Neither set attempted rhetorical criticism or evaluation that would penetrate beyond the notable southern orators' images as heroes. Leaving the myths untouched, the presentations merely confirmed existing impressions. It is doubtful whether any of these writings were based upon primary sources, careful research, or incisive analysis.

For almost thirty years after 1910, no one showed much interest in discussing southern public address. After the great flourish of writing between 1900 and 1910 on the subject, the teachers of southern literature almost completely ignored the subject. They became more sophisticated in their literary studies and found more southern writing worthy of critical comment and preservation. Of course, they had much more to take into account, because southern authors after 1920 attracted a wide readership, built national reputations, and produced a considerable body of work. In addition, it is entirely possible that the critics and teachers of literature became disgusted with the rhetorical excesses of the popular politicians or demagogues who spoke extemporaneously, played to the whims of the "red-necks," and indulged more in showmanship than in serious political speaking.

When speakers were cited in literary anthologies or in works on literature, it was their contributions to southern thought that usually received attention. A good case in point is Vernon L. Parrington's *Main Currents in American Thought*, which made a great impression on intellectual historians. Parrington devoted 136 pages to southern thought, taking notice of William Wirt, John C. Calhoun, Alexander H. Stephens, Hugh Swinton Legaré, and Jefferson Davis. Although he viewed them primarily as thinkers, his treatment did lend dignity to southern public address.[22]

In 1954, Jay B. Hubbell became the first person after Montrose Moses to turn out a significant anthology of southern writing. Following the lead of Parrington, Hubbell inserted brief discussions of many of the same men, but like his mentor he saw them as writers and thinkers, not as orators.[23]

What have the historians done about the concept of southern oratory? Although they have recognized and discussed individual speakers in many book-length biographies, in each case the author has seldom devoted more than a paragraph to the general subject. None has examined critically the notion of southern oratory. Francis P. Gaines suggested that William Garrott Brown first recognized the subject in

22. Vernon L. Parrington, *Main Currents in American Thought* (3 vols.; New York, 1927–30), II, 3–136.
23. Jay B. Hubbell, *The South in American Literature, 1607–1900* (Durham, N.C., 1954), 51–55, 117–22, 241, 265, 413–24.

The Lower South in American History, and Brown did indeed observe, "It is doubtful if there has ever been a society in which the orator counted for more than he did in the Cotton Kingdom."[24] But Brown considered only William L. Yancey; he had little to say about the larger subject.

Clement Eaton, who makes occasional reference to the subject, said in *A History of the Old South* that the "more florid tone" of southerners perhaps resulted from listening to "Indian eloquence." This conclusion represents extreme oversimplification. "Furthermore," he observed, "the florid type of oratory which was the fashion in the antebellum South was conditioned at least partly by the limited education of the audiences of farmers and villagers." In a second book, *Freedom of Thought in the Old South*, he gave one paragraph to the subject, saying in part, "The flowering of the romantic genius in the South occurred in the ornate style of oratory that won popular favor." To support this conclusion he cited three secondary sources: Francis Hall's *Travels in Canada and the United States* (1819), J. H. Ingraham's *The Sunny South or the Southerner at Home* (1860), and John Witherspoon Du Bose's manuscript on the life of Yancey. Such authors appear to have been no more than casual observers who chanced to include a paragraph or two on the subject.[25]

In *The Mind of the South*, W. J. Cash inserted fascinating little comments about southern rhetoric and the place of the southern orator in his analysis of the South's "established relationships and habits of thought, sentiment, prejudices, standards and values." His observations were intriguing and often insightful, but like much of what he wrote, he gave the reader little information about his sources. He definitely did confirm the long-held stereotypes. Frank Lawrence Owsley recognized the oral tradition as a significant part of the folk-

24. Francis Pendleton Gaines, *Southern Oratory: A Study in Idealism* (University, Ala., 1946); William Garrott Brown, *The Lower South in American History* (New York, 1902), 125.
25. Eaton, *History of the Old South*, 18; Eaton, *Freedom of Thought in the Old South*, 50–51.

ways of the southern yeoman farmer, but his observations about folk speaking, good as they are, are comparatively brief, touching mainly camp meetings, court days, and political rallies.[26]

In *The Growth of American Thought*, Merle Curti disposed of the subject in one short paragraph, without documentation. He said, "The Southern aristocracy found it . . . congenial and fitting to express the creative intellectual impulse in oratory." He admitted that some of the orations of John Randolph and John C. Calhoun were "rich in classical allusions and true to the Aristotelian pattern of oratorical composition . . . but most of the embroidered oratorical rhetoric was as ephemeral as it was florid." Curti did not offer a basis for his conclusion.[27]

Not one of the historians cited, or any others whose work I examined, presented a systematic study of what the orators said or the conditions under which speakers spoke. In the main, they based their conclusions upon scattered casual reports by observers who chanced to comment upon the subject in connection with discussions of such topics as the hysteria of a camp meeting, the drollness of country politicians, or the antics of a trial lawyer.

In recent years Francis Pendleton Gaines, in his little book *Southern Oratory: A Study in Idealism*, has been the only one to discuss the subject at length. Gaines argued that southern oratory owes its distinguishing quality to a thematic unity, that is, to its consideration of "the struggle for human freedom." To prove his thesis he considered Patrick Henry, Richard Henry Lee, John Randolph, John C. Calhoun, William Yancey, Henry Grady, and Woodrow Wilson. However, he left the old image of the southern orator unchallenged.[28]

In summary, the image of floridity and the belief that southern oratory is different from the speaking of other sections date back before

26. W. J. Cash, *The Mind of the South* (New York, 1941); Frank Lawrence Owsley, *Plain Folk of the Old South* (Baton Rouge, 1949).
27. Merle Curti, *The Growth of American Thought* (New York, 1943), 440.
28. Gaines, *Southern Oratory*.

the Civil War. The school readers reinforced and popularized the concept with brief eloquent passages from ceremonial speeches. They probably helped to perpetuate the myth by encouraging the students to imitate flowery models and expansive delivery.

It is evident that most early southern literary historians and anthologists contributed significantly to this image of southern oratory as well as to the formal study of the subject. They made available, particularly for the classroom, collections of speech excerpts. Often motivated by a sectional self-consciousness that craved recognition for everything "southern" and by a desire to keep alive southern regionalism, they tended to favor speeches of southern apologists and heroes. They chose brief, ornate, and figurative passages taken from the introductions and conclusions of commendations, eulogies, inaugural addresses, patriotic and ceremonial speeches, and literary lectures on southern themes. None of the works studied demonstrated a dimension sufficiently broad to represent the South's speaking in its entirety.

The southern cultural historians, doing little more than parrot the literary historians, continued to perpetuate an image based on little study or analysis. They gave their attention to frontier camp meetings, stump speaking, political harangues, and ceremonial speaking—often eulogies by southern heroes such as Patrick Henry, John Randolph of Roanoke, Robert Y. Hayne, William Yancey, and Seargent S. Prentiss. A study of southern oratory based upon apologists and heroes, portions of ceremonial speeches, secondary reports of casual observers, and sensational events such as frontier camp meetings and stump speeches, is bound to be myth-encrusted.

The Oral Tradition
in the Old South

Allen Tate, the distinguished critic and a born southerner, says that "the traditional southern mode of discourse presupposes somebody at the other end silently listening: it is the rhetorical mode. . . . The southerner always talks to somebody else, and this somebody else, after varying intervals, is given his turn; but . . . the typical southern conversation is not going anywhere, it is not about anything."[1] Now, when a southerner makes such a statement about the practices of his kinfolks, it would not be polite to object, but I do want to consider the influence of those whom Tate refers to as being "at the other end silently listening." The question that I wish to pose is, What influences did the southern listeners of the antebellum South have on "the traditional southern mode of discourse"?

Sometimes observers give too much attention to southern orators as causative forces without giving enough consideration to the influences and customs that motivated and molded them. It is easy for critics to become so entranced by colorful personalities and dramatic issues that they concentrate upon conventions and great meetings in Montgomery, Richmond, Charleston, and New Orleans instead of looking at the grass roots. Under the romantic spell of the Old Dominion or the Palmetto State, they may remember only the orators

1. Allen Tate, "A Southern Mode of Imagination," in *Studies in American Culture: Dominant Ideas and Images*, ed. Joseph J. Kwiat and Mary C. Turpie (Minneapolis, 1960), 100–101.

who were gentlemen of the class of John Randolph of Roanoke, Robert Y. Hayne, Richard Henry Lee, and William Wirt. Or they may praise only the planter-lawyer-politician who read Greek and Roman classics and Sir Walter Scott's Waverly novels and produced orations with the logic of a John C. Calhoun, the fire of a William L. Yancey, or the beauty of a Seargent S. Prentiss. At the other extreme, some historians and literary scholars have sought to rationalize the "flamboyant, ornate, spread-eagle type of oratory, superfluous in verbiage and all but barren of thought."[2] They have explained away that verbosity and grandiloquence as responses to the crudeness and ignorance of the populace.

Each view admittedly has merit, but it also represents an oversimplification. The first presents the speaker as a source of profound thoughts and great events; the second condemns him as a clever demagogue or con artist who hoodwinked the rustics with meaningless language, a powerful voice, and an ingratiating manner.

The purpose of this essay is to put the southern speaker into context, that is, to view him in the act of confronting friends, neighbors, and opponents and accommodating his speaking to prevailing frontier moods and preferences. The genre of southern oratory is a part of an oral tradition that had its beginnings at the family fireplace, revivals, court days, and hustings and that encompassed more than the few selected speeches preserved in anthologies and the flourishes of a few oratorical giants.

Where to start? At the outset some misconceptions about the people of the South need to be cleared away. A popular myth is that antebellum southerners fell into only two classes: planter aristocrats who lived on great plantations and owned hundreds of slaves, and poor whites, referred to variously as red-necks, crackers, hillbillies, sandhillers, and poor white trash, who lived far back in the red hills and piney woods.

2. Francis Pendleton Gaines, *Southern Oratory: A Study in Idealism* (University, Ala., 1946), 6.

To the contrary, many antebellum southerners did not fit into either category. In fact the vast majority were neither great planters nor poor whites but were in the wide middle group made up of yeoman farmers and a middle class that included professionals, storekeepers, schoolteachers, artisans, mechanics, tradesmen, and overseers. One authority suggests that these "plain folk" may not have been seriously backward when compared with the rural folk of the middle western states.[3]

In 1850 only one-fourth of southerners were slaveholders, and five-sevenths of these were yeoman farmers who owned fewer than 10 slaves. Unlike the planters, these simple people worked alongside their slaves in the fields. "To be of consequence a planter had to be master of 50 or more slaves," and less than 8,000 fell into this group. No more than 1,800 persons scattered over the whole South owned as many as 100 slaves. Many congressional districts had few slave-holders, and farmers with few slaves were in control. No more than 5 percent of southern whites were in the poor white group, at the lower end of the social scale.[4]

What do these facts suggest? Although the plantation culture dominated politics and attitudes and produced many of the leaders, southern speakers often faced audiences made up largely of yeoman farmers, middle-class artisans, and poor whites. Many affluent planters were the sons of, or started out as, common folk, and many had lived in log cabins. They often intermarried with yeoman families and participated in many activities with their poor neighbors. In background, taste, and sentiment, southerners, regardless of class, were much alike. In fact, in 1860 "much of the South was only one generation removed from frontier society."[5]

3. Frank Lawrence Owsley, *Plain Folk of the Old South* (Baton Rouge, 1949), 146–47.

4. Francis Butler Simkins and Charles Pierce Roland, *A History of the South* (4th ed.; New York, 1972), 132; Clement Eaton, "The Humor of the Southern Yeoman," *Sewanee Review*, XLIX (1941), 173.

5. Fletcher M. Green, *Democracy in the Old South and Other Essays* (Nashville, 1969), 80–83.

What else is known about these southern listeners? Outside a few centers such as New Orleans, Mobile, Charleston, Savannah, Louisville, and Richmond, the South was a rural society whose people were scattered over a vast land. In the 1840s the density of the white population was 95 per square mile in Massachusetts and 38 in Ohio. In comparison, it was 7 to 10 in states like Virginia and North Carolina and still more sparse, 4 to 10, in the lower South. Mississippi and Louisiana in 1850 could each claim no more than 45,000 white males of voting age. In Mississippi the two largest towns were Vicksburg (2,479) and Natchez (2,710), and in the entire state only 7 towns had a population over 500. In Louisiana only 8 towns had more than 1,000 people. In 1850 only 10 towns in Alabama had a population as large as 1,000, and the largest town was Mobile, with a population of 22,000. Over one-half of the 52 counties had no town of 500. In the Confederate South, only 6 cities had populations over 20,000.[6]

Farms and plantations often were miles apart. The neighboring village, sometimes the county seat, was often no more than a trading post, a tavern, a livery stable, and a church house or two located at a crossroads or a ferry. Isolated communities might be pulled together around crude little churches with their nearby graveyards. Away from the rivers, travel was slow, tortuous, and hazardous; a visit to a neighboring family, even five miles away, might involve great difficulty, with the ensuing stay lasting several days. As travelers like Frederick Law Olmsted made clear, the extending of hospitality was a necessity, because the occasional traveler had no other places to stay except in scattered farm or plantation homes, where the accommodations were often crude and not commodious.[7]

6. J. D. B. De Bow, *Statistical View of the United States: Being a Compendium of the Seventh Census* (Washington, D.C., 1854), 40, 366–448; Lewy Dorman, *Party Politics in Alabama from 1850 Through 1860* (Wetumpka, Ala., 1935), 15; Benjamin Burks Kendrick and Alex Arnett, *The South Looks at Its Past* (Chapel Hill, 1935).

7. Frederick Law Olmsted, *A Journey in the Seaboard Slave States* (New York, 1856), *passim*; Daniel R. Hundley, *Social Relations in Our Southern States*, ed. William J. Cooper, Jr. (Baton Rouge, 1979), 297–316.

It is obvious that for many rural southerners, life was often harsh, bleak, and lonely. Scattered as they were, they came into contact with few persons beyond their immediate families and near neighbors for days, weeks, or even months. News from outside was slow in coming, for few rural families had access to newspapers or magazines. Often they considered it a great treat to converse with a stranger, particularly if he was a good talker. Those unable to read were dependent for information and inspiration upon what they heard.[8]

Frank L. Owsley makes us aware of the "folkways" and "kinship ties" of the plain folk of the South. Bound together "by the ties of race, language, custom, tradition, and history," they were, he declares, "a genuine folk long before the Civil War. . . . The rural environment . . . where the whole family worked together, hunted together, went to church together, and expected to be buried together and to come to judgment together on the Last Day, helps explain the closely knit family group." The common ties extended beyond the immediate clan to friends and neighbors. The whole group built its existence around cooperative efforts: quilting bees, corn-huskings, harvests, logrollings, burning the woods, butcherings, and house raisings. Herein may perhaps be found the beginnings of the southerner's firm attachment to his local community that sociologists find still persists, his trust in close neighbors ("good ole boys") for counsel, his cordial hospitality, his cherishing of certain myths, and his pride in his kinfolks and their enclave.[9]

Now let us turn to the question of how this society developed an oral tradition. First, it is evident that orality was at the center of antebellum southern folk life. In many cabins storytelling was a ritual. Gathered around the fireplace in the evening, a family heard a grandfather or grandmother repeat legends of the old days, tales of spells,

8. Everett Dick, *The Dixie Frontier: A Social History* (New York, 1948), 324; Hamilton W. Pierson, *In the Brush of Old-Time Social, Political, and Religious Life in the Southwest* (New York, 1881), 47–59.

9. Owsley, *Plain Folk of the Old South*, 90, 95–132.

ghosts, and goblins, or accounts of great bear hunts and bloody feuds. Folk tales were passed down by word of mouth from generation to generation. W. J. Cash mentions that "the infant son of the planter" was brought up in an atmosphere "in which gray old black men were his most loved story-tellers." Many Uncle Remuses stirred the imaginations of little boys and made characters like Brer Rabbit and Brer Fox come to life. Such stories later found wider circulation through the help of writers like Joel Chandler Harris who had long memories, keen ears for dialect, and a good sense of the dramatic.[10]

But conversation and storytelling had a much broader stage than the cabin and plantation. Storytelling became standard practice at social gatherings. When the women got together, especially after church, "they chatted about their family, their gardens, flowers, chickens, clothes and the forthcoming weddings and planned dinners and quilting." Trips to market towns to buy supplies, trade horses, pass the jug, play the fiddle and banjo, or frolic at a hoedown also provided opportunities, especially for the menfolk, to exchange information, visit, gossip, and argue politics. The great storytellers became favorite companions who attracted eager listeners. And as Owsley says, no occasion was "permitted to come to an end without tall tales and spicy anecdotes going their rounds."[11]

"Since such yarns were comic," Walter Blair suggests, "it was not surprising that a large share of that humor used as its substance the stuff of current tales." Many of them first found their way into print through the efforts of journalists seeking to enliven the newspapers and lawyers swapping stories to entertain each other. These often-told tales became the sources and inspiration for such writers as Davy Crockett (*A Narrative of the Life of David Crockett, of the State of Tennessee*, 1834), Augustus B. Longstreet (*Georgia Scenes*, 1835), Henry Clay Lewis (who, under the pseudonym of Madison Tensas, wrote *Odd Leaves from the Life of a Louisiana Swamp Doctor*, 1850), Thomas Bangs

10. W. J. Cash, *The Mind of the South* (New York, 1941), 49; Alice Walker, "Uncle Remus: No Friend of Mind," *Southern Exposure*, IX (Summer, 1981), 29–31.
11. Owsley, *Plain Folk of the Old South*, 97.

Thorpe (*The Mysteries of the Backwoods*, 1846), Joseph G. Baldwin (*The Flush Times of Alabama and Mississippi*, 1853), and George Washington Harris (*Sut Lovingood Yarns by a "Nat'ral Born Durn'd Fool,"* 1867). [12]

Many southern politicians built their speaking around their storytelling. Zebulon Vance (1830–1894) of North Carolina became known for his salty stories, which in fact were so earthy that many were never published. Later, Private John Allen of Mississippi, Thomas Heflin of Alabama, and Huey P. Long of Louisiana became famous for their effective use of humor. [13]

A second important factor in the development of the oral tradition in the South was religion. Religious activities had a marked influence on the tastes of southern listeners. The rural church became the gathering place where relatives and neighbors assembled to visit, exchange views, and keep friendships alive. Before church houses were built, groups met in cabins to hear itinerant preachers. On a weekend, they sometimes congregated at what one writer called "basket-meetings" at convenient clearings in the "tall and dense, unbroken forests." Reminiscing about her experiences in early Georgia, Emily Burke, a New England schoolteacher, spoke of going to a rural meeting where persons from "all the plantations" in the section came from as far as "five, ten, or fifteen miles." She recalled that the building was "merely frame covered slightly with boards . . . having neither bell, cupola or glass windows; the most that can be said of it is that it was a shelter." [14]

12. Walter Blair, "Traditions in Southern Humor," *American Quarterly*, V (1953), 135; Arlin Turner, "Realism and Fantasy in Southern Humor," *Georgia Review*, XII (1958), 451–97; John K. Bettersworth, "The Humor of the Old Southwest: Yesterday and Today," *Mississippi Quarterly*, XVII (1969), 88–94.

13. Franklin R. Shirley, *Zebulon Vance: Tarheel Spokesman* (Charlotte, 1962); Loren Reid, "Private John Allen: A Humorist in Politics," *Quarterly Journal of Speech*, XXVIII (1942), 414–21; G. Allan Yeomans, "Southern Oratory and the Art of Storytelling: A Case Study," *Southern Speech Journal*, XXXII (1967), 251–60.

14. Pierson, *In the Brush of Old-Time Social, Political, and Religious Life in the Southwest*, 60–61; Emily Burke, *Reminiscences of Georgia* (Oberlin, Ohio, 1850), 144–49.

Sunday services, prayer meetings, baptisms, weddings, and funerals brought singing, praying, and preaching, but also what many clergymen considered frivolous socializing. In stern admonition, the Reverend Nathan S. S. Beman, a preacher at Mount Zion, Georgia, warned his congregation: "Visiting on the Sabbath, particularly after public worship, is calculated to destroy the good effects of preaching. All the solemnity inspired in the house of God is often in a single hour overwhelmed and lost amid the convivial gaiety and mirth which pervade the social circle." [15]

After crops were laid by, a family might take a break and travel many miles to attend a revival or a camp meeting, perhaps staying a week or more. These carnivals would sometimes attract hundreds and even thousands. For example, the Cane Ridge revival in eastern Kentucky in 1800 drew crowds estimated at over twenty thousand. Tent villages, sometimes formally arranged and administered, sprang up. Tradesmen came to hawk their wares. The primitive, hellfire-and-brimstone preachers, often from several denominations, would sometimes excoriate sin and Satan from midmorning until far into the torch-lighted night; four or five might hold forth at the same time at various places on the vast campground. Many sinners were not as interested in discussion of Scripture as they were in "feeling the Spirit," which was reflected in shouting, barking, praying, singing, and crying for God's mercy. Primitive frenzy and hysteria were manifest in what was often called "exercises": fainting, jerks, laughter, moaning, and dancing. In the words of one observer, those moved mistook "animal excitement for holy ecstacy." Only a persistent, leather-lunged preacher or circuit rider could cope with the wilderness, the competition from other soul savers, the antics of the rowdies, and the mass hysteria of the communicants. Indeed, these meetings brought more than religion; they brought socializing and excitement and made rural people forget their rough and drab lives. [16]

15. Owen Peterson, "Nathan S. S. Beman at Mt. Zion," *Georgia Historical Quarterly*, XLIX (1965), 163. Beman was the stepfather of William L. Yancey.

16. Owsley, *Plain Folk of the Old South*, 96–103; W. H. Sparks, *The Memories of*

Out of this religious ferment arose numerous competing sects that proselytized in order to gather congregations and build substantial church houses—frequently three or four in a growing village. The camp meetings often settled in fixed locations with permanent layouts and tabernacles. Congregations promoted sobriety through church trials and the penalty of excommunication for offenses such as drunkenness, sexual immorality, gambling, dancing, abuse of family members, and unorthodoxy. They established academies and schools, particularly to train their ministers.

The clergy lost a little of their fire and roughness and became better educated and more urbane. Like the lawyers, they were often extremely argumentative, engaging each other in doctrinal debates that attracted eager listeners and were sometimes published in flourishing religious journals. As a part of their preaching, they rationalized slavery, created a "religiously solid South" and contributed to the growth of southern nationalism. Churchgoing and orthodoxy evolved as important characteristics of southerners of all classes.[17] At the heart of these religious activities was the binding force of the preacher, who lived by the oral mode.

Third, the lawyers and courts became important ingredients in the development of the oral tradition. As an escape from tedium, spectators often crowded into courtrooms, regarding them as a kind of theater. Hamilton W. Pierson wrote that a "petty lawsuit" often brought "together the most of the people in the neighborhood to hear . . . the opposing . . . lawyers. County and circuit-court days were the great days of the year, when the people . . . hour after hour, and day after day, listened to the speeches." He reported that "in cases of

---

Fifty Years (Philadelphia, 1882), 113–16; Guion Griffis Johnson, *Ante-Bellum North Carolina* (Chapel Hill, 1937), 377–409; Evan Ulrey, "The Preaching of Barton Warren Stone" (Ph.D. dissertation, Louisiana State University, 1964).

17. Simkins and Roland, *A History of the South*, 158; John McCardell, *The Idea of a Southern Nation: Southern Nationalists and Southern Nationalism, 1830–1860* (New York, 1979), 177–226.

unusual interest and excitement, such as a murder trial," even the wives and daughters turned out to hear the oratory.[18]

Southerners were often contentious and liked to haul each other into court. Joseph G. Baldwin said that after the crash of 1837 in Sumpter County, Alabama, in one year "some four or five thousand suits, in the common law courts alone, were brought." He added that "the white suable population . . . was then some 2,400 men." As a young lawyer in Mississippi in the 1830s, Reuben Davis brought 480 cases to circuit court of Monroe County in one term, and in a four-year period he "put by a surplus of twenty thousand dollars." He recalled that "the major part of criminal cases except misdemeanors were for killings or assault with intent to kill," and the defense was usually based upon "points of chivalry."[19]

Contemporary accounts suggest that the lawyers fascinated the rural folk with wit, repartee, and antics. Of course, these "lawyer-lings," traveling their circuits with their libraries and their clothes in their saddlebags, knew that quick tongues were necessary if they were to attract clients. With little or no preparation, they were often in court representing recently acquired clients the same day they were engaged or the one following. "Readiness, precision, plainness, perti-nency, knowledge of law, and a short hand method of getting at and getting through with a case," according to Baldwin, "were the char-acteristics and desiderata of the profession." But knowing that court-room flourishes increased their stature, they undoubtedly played sometimes as much to the spectators as to the judge and jury. They became adept at handling the give-and-take of the unexpected and probably substituted bombast for argument.

The popularity of the legal profession suggests another dimension of the oral tradition. Young men looked upon the law as "the surest

18. Pierson, *In the Brush of Old-Time Social, Political, and Religious Life in the Southwest*, 162.

19. Joseph G. Baldwin, *The Flush Times of Alabama and Mississippi* (New York, 1957), 175; Reuben Davis, *Recollections of Mississippi and Mississippians* (Boston, 1891), 57.

stepping stone to political preferment." Thomas Nelson Page explained that a native young southerner "who was too poor to live without work, or too ambitious to be contented with his plantation, devoted himself to the learned professions—the law being the most desirable as offering the best opportunity for forensic display."[20] The ties between the lawyers and planters were strong, for after acquiring a legal education, a young lawyer—often the son of a middle-class family or a Yankee who had come south to seek his fortune—would acquire a plantation and enter the upper class. Of course, the easiest way to travel this road was to marry a planter's daughter.

Although the clique of large planters set "the dominant tone in society, the lawyers generally took the lead in intellectual matters." Where better to master the art of eloquence than in the law, which went hand in hand with politics and oratory.[21] Some of the strongest defenders of the southern way of life were lawyers who had moved upward on the social scale. No better proof of the importance of legal training as a stepping-stone to recognition and admittance to the planter class can be offered than the long list of prominent antebellum southern lawyers who moved upward to leadership. Foremost were Judah P. Benjamin, John C. Calhoun, Henry Clay, Henry S. Foote, Patrick Henry, Henry W. Hilliard, Hugh S. Legaré, William C. Preston, Seargent S. Prentiss, John A. Quitman, Alexander H. Stephens, Pierre Soulé, William Wirt, William L. Yancey, and on and on.

Fourth, politicking was a significant aspect of the oral tradition in the antebellum South. Complaining that "the South suffered from too much campaigning," one writer suggested that interest in politics "was as strong with the humblest citizen as with the most prominent;

20. Baldwin, *Flush Times*, 176; Thomas Nelson Page, *The Old South: Essays, Social and Political* (New York, 1892), 238.

21. William Garrott Brown, *The Lower South in American History* (New York, 1902), 8, 18, 14; Davis, *Recollections*, 363; Jay B. Hubbell, *The South in American Literature, 1607–1900* (Durham, N.C., 1954), 215.

the joint debates and the oratory at militia musters and at monthly court not only kept alive from year to year the excitement among those who welcomed any opportunity to mingle with their fellows, but supplemented the small circulation of the press and the inability of many voters to read."[22]

The people's enthusiasm for the hustings almost matched their excitement at revivals and camp meetings. Reuben Davis, a successful lawyer and politician of Monroe County, Mississippi, provided a view of the political climate when he recounted his experiences in the 1840 presidential campaign, which he said was "in every aspect . . . an extraordinary one. . . . There were public speeches everywhere. Great barbecues succeeded each other and were attended by multitudes, who thronged to the appointed place in wagons and carriages, on foot and on horseback; travelling for miles to enjoy these social and political festivals. . . . The more rigid moralist may have been scandalized by the spectacle of whole communities given up to wild days of feasting, speech-making, music, dancing and drinking, with, perhaps, rough words now and then and an honest hand to hand fight when debate was angry and the blood hot."

Davis wrote enthusiastically about a great political safari from Monroe County in east central Mississippi to Nashville, Tennessee.

> It was proposed that a meeting of the people of the West and South should be held at Nashville, Tenn., during the month of August. . . . It was agreed that a hundred men should be appointed as a committee to represent Monroe County at this meeting. I was one of the hundred selected, and we went to work with zealous preparation for the journey.
>
> A new wagon was chosen and gayly painted. It was appropriately fitted up with a neatly built log cabin and the typical barrel of hard cider, not forgetting sundry coon-skins among the adorning banners. Six of the finest horses in market were harnessed to this wagon, and the hundred delegates formed a mounted escort for it. We had tents and provisions with us, a band of music, and a retinue of negro men and boys, who were enchanted that their service made it necessary to follow

22. Edward Ingle, *Southern Sidelights* (New York, 1896), 39.

their masters on such an expedition. . . . We travelled about fifteen miles a day, stopping at every crossroad to meet the people who came out to greet us. Wherever we tarried, there was music and speaking. The men brought out their best liquors, and the women their choicest dainties for our refreshment. . . . When we came to the larger towns and villages, committees were ready to receive us, and preparations made for elaborate entertainment. It was many long summer days before we reached Nashville. . . . Thousands were in advance of us, and it was estimated that more than a hundred thousand were present on the appointed day. Many speakers, of more or less celebrity, were ready to address the people from various stands, chief among them Henry Clay, and Thomas Corwin of Ohio.

The "great enjoyment and festivity" at these occasions is suggested in Davis' account of an 1844 rally at Davis Mills, fifteen miles north of Holly Springs, on the Tennessee border.

> For miles around the appointed place, and for weeks before the appointed time, the notable house keepers . . . were busy in preparing food. . . . The long tables groaned under the weight of substantial viands and tempting dainties, and the good ladies heaped the plates for every guest. Lads and lassies came out to enjoy the frolic and even children were brought to see the great men of the day. . . . There were negroes in abundance. . . . In every neighborhood there were always certain old negro cooks who had special secrets in the management of barbecued meats, and these were always installed chiefs of that department. . . . Only those who can remember the old South in its glory can have an adequate idea of a big barbecue in 1844.[23]

Often a campaign resolved itself into an extensive itinerary involving a series of joint debates, much like the Lincoln-Douglas contest of 1858 in Illinois. The candidates, or the electors acting as surrogates, traveled together, matching wits at each stop. In 1839, James K. Polk of Tennessee delivered 43 scheduled and numerous impromptu speeches over a period of 2 months, riding horseback over 1,300 miles. In 1843, when he lost, Polk and his opponent crisscrossed

23. Davis, *Recollections*, 111–14, 197–98.

Tennessee in a 4-month period on an itinerary of 2,300 miles, speaking 5 or 6 hours a day.

The campaigners usually engaged in much handshaking, drinking, clowning, and storytelling, and many face-to-face exchanges. After a rally, the party faithful might crowd into a local tavern for more discussion and, of course, more drinking. A given rally might last four or more hours and include speeches by the principals and local personalities, carefully contrived questions, rejoinders, repartee, side comments, and responses from the onlookers.[24]

Henry S. Foote recalled engaging in a debate with Seargent S. Prentiss at Gallatin, Tennessee, in 1840 that "continued for eleven hours; the speeches being delivered alternatively. . . . Not a word of discourtesy was spoken during this memorable day and night by either of us; we slept in a little log tavern at Gallatin and travelled in company the next day, lunching on the roadside before we parted company for our respective homes."[25]

Office seekers from the local level all the way up to the United States Congress knew that they had to get out and meet the voters in order to win; consequently, they made extensive canvasses even into the backcountry. Hamilton W. Pierson reported that "no class of people in the Southwest were so omnipresent as office seeking politicians. I have visited no neighborhood so remote, no valley so deep, no mountain so high, that the secluded cabins had not been honored by visits of aspiring politicians, eager to secure the votes of their 'sovereign' occupants."[26]

Did the people influence the mode of speaking? Pierson suggested that the "fondness of the people for public discussion, and speeches

24. *Ibid.*, 193–94; William J. Cooper, Jr., *The South and the Politics of Slavery, 1828–1856* (Baton Rouge, 1978), 32–42; Robert G. Gunderson, "The Southern Whigs," in *Oratory in the Old South*, ed. Waldo W. Braden (Baton Rouge, 1970), 104–41.

25. Henry S. Foote, *Casket of Reminiscences* (New York, 1968), 191.

26. Pierson, *In the Brush of Old-Time Social, Political, and Religious Life in the Southwest*, 130. See also Paul H. Buck, "The Poor Whites of the Ante-bellum South," *American Historical Review*, XXXI (1925), 44–54.

upon all sorts of subjects," along with "the remarkable attention" given the speakers and "the visible effects produced by their words," stimulated the orators "to draw out all their powers." This situation, Pierson believed, did "much to develop the peculiar and often very remarkable oratory that prevailed." Although the speakers molded the minds and opinions of the people, at the same time the people molded the speakers' peculiar style of oratory. They acted upon, and reacted to, each other.[27]

The socializing, feasting, merriment, pageantry, spectacle, ritual, arguing, and orating were dramatic, bringing rural citizens out of isolation and releasing tension. These events became a contact with the outside world, developed leaders and heroes, and strengthened the common bonds that made southerners into what Owsley speaks of as "common folk."

The oral tradition in the South found its most eloquent manifestation on those special days that required expressions of pride and thankfulness. Southerners, like other Americans, expressed their greatest enthusiasm through displays of elegant or contrived rhetoric, or what has been called "pure oratory."

They especially enjoyed rip-roaring Fourth of July celebrations, at first mainly in the larger towns but later also in the villages. On other occasions they turned out from far and near to commemorate notable events: anniversaries of historic events or of births and deaths of heroes such as George Washington and Thomas Jefferson, visits by former U.S. presidents or by notables such as Edward Everett, Henry Clay, or Daniel Webster, or the completions of railroads, courthouses, or churches. In 1825 the citizens of North Carolina became greatly excited over the visit of Lafayette to the Old North State.[28]

27. Pierson, *In the Brush of Old-Time Social, Political, and Religious Life in the Southwest*, 162–63; Davis, *Recollections*, 83.

28. Johnson, *Ante-Bellum North Carolina*, 140–50; Fletcher M. Green, "Listen to the Eagle Scream: One Hundred Years of the Fourth of July in North Carolina (1776–1876)," *North Carolina Historical Review*, XXX (1954), 295–320, 529–49.

After 1820, in many communities the celebration of the signing of the Declaration of Independence developed into a ritual that included the ringing of church bells, the firing of cannons and volleys of musket fire, a parade of military units and citizens, and, most important, an assembly at the courthouse or a church for a prayer, the reading of the Declaration, and the address of the day by an orator who could make the "eagle scream" and the flag flutter. Sometimes groups found ways to use the Fourth to promote their special causes, which might be the Sunday school, the temperance crusade, female education, or a political campaign. Robert Barnwell Rhett used a celebration at Walterborough, South Carolina, on July 4, 1832, to deliver one of his important addresses on nullification.[29]

In the larger cities, organizations such as fraternal orders, lyceums, literary clubs, debating societies, mechanics' associations, library associations, temperance societies, and benevolent societies attempted to foster education, culture, reform, and other worthy causes through public meetings, lectures, and formal addresses. They were often able to enlist exceptional local talent and to attract distinguished speakers from outside. The People's Lyceum in New Orleans, for example, presented some of the most prominent citizens of the city and the nation on the lecture platform.[30]

It was on these ceremonial occasions that the demonstrative orators engaged in their most grandiloquent presentations. A typical speech "was extravagant and studded with over-statement. It was hortatory and evangelistic. It was a mixture of uplift, 'vision' rodomontade, gasconade, salty common sense, and broad and bucolic humor." William G. Carleton nominates as "the 'purest' of the 'pure orators'. . . . William C. Preston and Hugh S. Legaré of South Carolina and S. S. Prentiss of Mississippi."[31] Such orators received rapt attention when-

29. H. Hardy Perritt, "Robert Barnwell Rhett: Prophet of Resistance, 1828–1834," *Southern Speech Journal*, XXI (1955), 108–11.

30. Waldo W. Braden, "Lecturing in New Orleans, 1840–1850," *Southern Studies*, XVII (1978), 433–46; Johnson, *Ante-Bellum North Carolina*, 140–50, 162–74.

31. William G. Carleton, "The Celebrity Cult a Century Ago," *Georgia Review*, XIV (1960), 133–42.

ever they spoke, fascinating not only the plain folk but also other speakers, who listened with awe and envy.[32] For this reason much of the "pure oratory," often presented from carefully prepared manuscripts or memorized, has been preserved in anthologies and has led many to conclude that it was representative of all the southern speaking of the time. But perhaps it was no more typical in the South than it was elsewhere.[33]

Another reflection of the oral tradition in the South was the popularity of literary societies and school exhibitions at academies and colleges. Can you imagine schoolboys devoting their spare time to debating, declaiming, and orating? Around 1850, in most of the 120 colleges of the South, the literary societies were the principal authorized extracurricular activity and great stimulators of intellectual discussions, as well as the assemblers of the first campus libraries.[34]

Each campus had two or more of these secret groups; many had their own buildings, some of which are still standing today. Former members took pride in their old school ties, returning on occasion to participate in the speaking. For example, when the Demosthenians of Franklin College (University of Georgia) held their first meeting in their newly erected hall, John C. Calhoun presided, assisted by Moses Waddell, who had been president of the school from 1819 to 1829. Other distinguished guests included Joseph Henry Lumpkin (a lawyer and later justice of the first supreme court of Georgia) and Augustus Baldwin Longstreet (lawyer, judge, clergyman, author, and president of Emory and the University of Mississippi). Howell Cobb, a member at the time, delivered an oration.[35] The "big man on

32. This conclusion about speakers in the audiences is supported by what orators of the time said about each other. See Baldwin, *Flush Times*, 144–62; Foote, *Casket of Reminiscences*, 428–35; Sparks, *The Memories of Fifty Years*, 343–72.

33. Barnet Baskerville, "19th Century Burlesque of Oratory," *American Quarterly*, XX (1968), 726–43.

34. Frank Davis, "The Literary Societies of Selected State Universities of the Lower South" (Ph.D. dissertation, Louisiana State University, 1949); E. Merton Coulter, *College Life in the Old South* (New York, 1928), Chap. VI.

35. Coulter, *College Life in the Old South*, 105.

campus" in those days was often the one thought to be the most eloquent or chosen to deliver an oration at commencement time. On Saturdays, from about nine o'clock in the morning until well into the night, young southerners discussed all manner of subjects, from the most ridiculous to the most serious, ranging over history, literature, philosophy, logic, religion, and current affairs.

For example, the Demosthenians of Franklin College considered in their very first debate, on February 23, 1803, the question, "Is monarchial government preferable to the republican?" The Clariosophic Society of South Carolina College debated the following questions: "Should the United States favor Napoleon?" (1811), "In view of international disputes should the United States navy be increased?" (1812), and "Will England or France become greater?" (1814). Not always choosing such weighty questions, the Demosthenians, on February 4, 1846, debated the question, "Are the intellectual capacities of males superior to those of females?" The youthful male chauvinists of the day won the contest by a vote of 20–8. The boys of the Phi Kappa Society (also of Franklin College) took a slightly different approach, deciding against the affirmative on the question, "Should seduction mean marriage?" (May 14, 1842). On April 3, 1851, the affirmative won on the question, "Are men always to chase?" The young debaters, influenced by contemporary attitudes, sometimes looked into matters touching slavery in such topics as "Should the slave trade be reopened?" "Is the African in possession of a soul?" and "Is the cost of slavery too high?"

It would be fascinating to know what was actually said in these and the thousands of other debates by young southerners. But unfortunately, since the meetings were secret, all that remain in the record books are lists of innumerable topics, the votes taken, and the names of those who participated.[36]

Likewise, commencements, final examinations, and exhibitions at

36. In his study of literary societies in the state colleges of South Carolina, Georgia, Alabama, and Mississippi, Frank Davis listed hundreds of propositions, of which those given here are a few. See Davis, "The Literary Societies of Selected State Universities," 183n, 223n.

the end of the term attracted large gatherings of parents and well-wishers to the many private academies as well as to the colleges. One writer, reporting on the year-end school exhibitions, recollected the interest that the communities took in these activities during the first half of the nineteenth century in middle Georgia.

Whenever a master remained until the end of the spring term, it closed with an examination of the pupils on the last day and what was called an "exhibition" at night. A rude platform was built in front of the door, and an arbor covered with branches of trees extended far out. Many hundreds attended the examinations and many more the exhibition. To the latter people came from all distances up to 10 and 15 miles, often to the number of two and three thousand, and it was curious to see the interest taken in these exercises by persons.[37]

Parents, even those with little education, wanted their sons well trained, and they equated a good education with the ability to mount the platform and deliver a stirring oration. Although the visitors may not have always understood much of the subject matter, they took pride in hearing the children recite and orate. As they listened, they probably fantasized that they were hearing a future governor or senator. And in truth, many future political greats did get their starts on these platforms.

Another hint of the pervasiveness of the oral tradition is a negative one. The slowness of the region to produce noteworthy writers and poets of distinction has been explained by pointing to the southerner's preference for politics and the spoken word. "Eloquence promised more to southern youth than literary pursuits," concluded one scholar. William Gilmore Simms, who struggled to improve the southern literary reputation and often complained in print that his efforts were not appreciated, blamed the rural nature of the South for

37. Richard Malcolm Johnston, "Early Educational Life in Middle Georgia," in U.S. Department of the Interior, Bureau of Education, *Report of the Commissioner of Education for Year 1894–95* (2 vols.; 1896), II, 1699–1733.

the literary backwardness. Simms claimed, "No purely agricultural people, anywhere, has ever produced a national literature; has ever triumphed in the Arts, belles letters, or the Drama; though they have produced great orators, politicians, warriors, and even philosophers." Allen Tate reinforced this view: "If we say that the old southern mind was rhetorical we must add that our access to it must be through its public phase, which was almost exclusively political." Virginius Dabney, the distinguished editor, suggested that the southerner's "intense desire to master the spoken word was one of the factors in his neglect of the profession of letters. The cherished ambition of almost every young Southerner was for a public rather than a literary career." [38]

Some literary critics have argued that an oratorical quality tainted southern literary attempts. They have declared southern writing prior to 1920 to be polemic, didactic, overindulgent, pseudoromantic, declamatory, and excessively ornate. Not many persons except the authors of that period would deny many of these charges.

But more recently, scholars have concluded that the rhetorical slant was not all bad, for they have commended the oral qualities in the writing of Edgar Allan Poe, Mark Twain, Thomas Wolfe, Eudora Welty, and William Faulkner. They point out that such writers demonstrated a feeling for orality in their dialogue, in their accounts of folk life, and in their prose rhythms. For example, Arlin Turner suggests that Twain had an "infallible ear for oral speech." Robert B. Heilman observes that one of the aspects of the "southern temperament" is "a sense of the ornamental or the rhetorical bent." In a discussion of novelists Robert Penn Warren and William Faulkner, Heilman says, "There is a special awareness of the verbal medium, a disposition to elaborate and amplify as a fundamental mode of com-

38. Jay B. Hubbell, "Literary Nationalism in the Old South," in *American Studies in Honor of William Kenneth Boyd*, ed. David Kelly Jackson (Durham, N.C., 1940), 181; William Gilmore Simms, "Literary Prospects of the South," *Russell's Magazine*, III (June, 1858), 194; Tate, "A Southern Mode of Imagination," 100–101; Virginius Dabney, *Liberalism in the South* (Chapel Hill, 1932), 80–81.

munication, a willingness to utilize the rich and the rhythmical, an instinctive exploration of the stylistic instrument to the ultimate point at which one senses something of the supererogatory but not yet the excessive or obtrusive." [39]

How do these threads tie together? Like the Indian fighter, the hunter, and the military hero, the masters of the oral medium became folk heroes. Confirming this conclusion, Reuben Davis spoke of the "universal enjoyment of public speaking" as "one of the most remarkable characteristics of the Southern people before the war." As a consequence, he said, "the art of fluent speaking was largely cultivated, and a man could hope for little success in public life unless he possessed that faculty in some degree. Another consequence was that there was never a people better educated on political questions than the Southerners of that day." Perhaps Davis claimed a little too much for the educational function of the speaking, but he was certainly right about the pervasiveness of the oral tradition. [40]

When they assembled, antebellum southerners sometimes yielded to the emotions of the revivals, the drama of the courtrooms, the excitement of the rally, and the inspiration of special occasions. As an escape from the loneliness of their drab lives, they often let rowdiness and boisterousness creep into their work, their play, their creative efforts, and naturally their speaking. In this context those storytellers, conversationalists, ministers, lawyers, and public men who could master the crowds met what Cash called the "primary standard . . . the *sine qua non* of leadership." [41]

Because newspapers did not circulate widely and many people could not read, speakers became great sources of information and entertainment as well as inspiration. The result was that listeners

39. Turner, "Realism and Fantasy in Southern Humor," 457; Robert B. Heilman, "The Southern Temper," in *Southern Renascence*, ed. Louis D. Rubin, Jr., and Robert D. Jacobs (Baltimore, 1953), 9.

40. Davis, *Recollections*, 69.

41. Cash, *The Mind of the South*, 51.

cultivated a fondness for the medium that brought "the immediate and directly observable satisfactions of speech rather than the more remote ones of writing."[42] Many speakers developed excesses in style and manner in response to feedback from listeners who became attentive, entranced, and amused. With little basis for making critical rhetorical judgments, these plain listeners exercised little restraint over the developing oral tradition of the South.

Antebellum southerners preferred having problems talked out, enjoyed face-to-face encounters, and took pleasure in hearing lawyers, preachers, and politicians let loose their oratorical devices. Such listeners gained much information, understanding, and entertainment in the public forum. In turn, they provided an atmosphere that encouraged the developing mode of southern rhetoric.

42. *Ibid.*, 97.

⦙⦙⦙ III ⦙⦙⦙

The 1860 Election Campaign
in Western Tennessee

In the presidential election of 1860, the Douglas Democrats, the Breckinridge Democrats, and the Constitutional Unionists campaigned vigorously in Memphis, Tennessee. Local politicians received substantial help from nationally known speakers who found profit and pleasure in speaking at this crossroads of railroad and river. Before the end of the canvass, William L. Yancey, Jefferson Davis, Louis T. Wigfall, L. Q. C. Lamar, William Sharkey, Andrew Johnson, Stephen A. Douglas, and many lesser lights had displayed their rhetorical wares before the Memphis voters. Few places in the nation were treated to more varied and colorful political oratory.

Why was this area important? Many crosscurrents of conflicting interests and diverse attitudes swirled through this region. Merchants, bankers, and cotton factors maintained firm ties with the North and West as well as with the downriver interests. They were alarmed by threats to the Union, because they had a valuable trade and held dreams of a greater city. Plantation owners sympathized with slavocracy, viewed with passion Yankee interference with slavery, and imagined a great conspiracy to take away their property. They felt a kinship with planters of the Deep South. The foreign-born residents, mainly Irish and Germans, some 30 percent of the population, were much opposed to the Constitutional Unionists, who were tainted with Know-Nothingism; consequently, they became fair game for the warring Democrats.

The result was a delicate balance between Whigs and Democrats. Even in years when the Democrats were united, they had difficulty defeating their old Whig foes, who were particularly strong in the plantation areas of the Tenth Congressional District, in the southwest corner of the state (Fayette, Hardeman, Haywood, Madison, and Shelby counties). In 1860 the split between the Douglasites and southern bolters cast doubt upon the outcome of the election. The loss of a single district in Tennessee would be enough to give the state to the Constitutional Unionists.

In spite of hot summer weather, the news of the national political conventions stirred Memphis party men to action. The rejuvenated Whigs, or Constitutional Unionists, soon perfected a local organization and held a rally to ratify the nomination of Bell and Everett. Tennessee Whigs, foremost nationally in organizing the new party and in nominating the Tennessee senator, had little difficulty developing local groups throughout the state, including the southwest. In Memphis they promoted the Central Union Club, the Young Men's Bell and Everett Club, and groups in the First, Second, Sixth, Seventh, and Eighth wards. Throughout the period they relied mostly upon local speakers, usually four or five at a meeting. In addition, they vented enthusiasm through singing, torchlight processions, basket dinners, pole-raisings, and incessant bell-ringing in honor of John Bell.[1]

The Democrats had difficulty deciding which faction of the Democracy should control the state. When Yancey and other "seceders" walked out of the Charleston convention in late April, the Tennessee delegates, although sympathetic, refused to bolt. At the Baltimore convention, nineteen of the twenty-four Tennessee delegates withdrew when the contested Douglas delegates of Louisiana and Alabama were seated. These bolters helped nominate Breckinridge and Lane. Without difficulty this wing gained the support of most of the Democratic newspapers of Tennessee and most of the district organizations.

1. Joseph Howard Parks, *John Bell of Tennessee* (Baton Rouge, 1950), 339–60; Memphis *Enquirer*, July 11, 1860.

But in the Tenth Congressional District and in northern Mississippi and eastern Arkansas, the admirers of Douglas resisted stubbornly. The Memphis *Appeal*, the largest paper in west Tennessee, came out for the Little Giant.[2] Ratification meetings for him were numerous. In Memphis, on July 5, two days after one faction approved the nomination of Breckinridge and Lane, a second group countered with a ratification meeting for Douglas. The *Appeal* estimated the attendance at 3,500, while the *Avalanche* put the number between 1,200 and 1,500. Samuel P. Walker reported to Douglas that this rally was "the largest and most enthusiastic" he had ever seen in Memphis. At the district convention, which assembled at the Exchange Building on July 11, 1860, the Breckinridge Democrats apparently lacked sufficient strength to risk a showdown; consequently, without a fight they withdrew to the Odd Fellows Hall. An apologist explained that the bolters, not wishing to create "ill feeling," voluntarily chose to move. If this explanation was true, it was the only time during the four-month campaign that either faction attempted to avoid "ill feeling."[3]

Each wing set up a local organization. Less active than either of their rivals, Breckinridge Democrats worked through two clubs, the Shelby County Democrats Association and the Young Men's Democratic Association. The Douglas Democrats, rivaling the Bellites in enthusiasm, promoted seven groups: the Democratic Association of Shelby County, the German Douglas Club, the Young Men's Little Giant Club, the Mechanics Club, the Bluff City Club, the Chelsea

2. The *Appeal* was published daily, triweekly, and weekly. During the campaign the *Weekly Appeal*, with a circulation of 5,144, was devoted entirely to politics. Other Douglas papers in the Tenth District were the Somerville *Democrat*, the Bolivar *Democrat*, and the Grand Junction *Quid Nunc* (Memphis *Weekly Appeal*, July 18, 1860).

3. Memphis *Avalanche*, July 4, 18, 1860; Memphis *Daily Appeal*, July 8, 1860; Samuel P. Walker to Stephen A. Douglas, July 9, 1860, W. L. Green to Douglas, July 17, 1860, both in Stephen A. Douglas Papers, University of Chicago Library, Chicago; Memphis *Weekly Appeal*, July 18, 1860.

Club, and the South Memphis Club. These groups kept their partisans busy with nightly rallies, serenades, torchlight parades, and barbecues.

By late July, the Breckinridge forces had abandoned hope of gaining undisputed control of the party organization. The Douglasites, under competent leadership and cheered on by the *Appeal*, continued to be aggressive and persistent. The anti-Douglas forces feared that this disaffection in a district that had previously contributed majorities to the Democrats would tip the delicate balance in favor of Bell and thereby cost them the state.

One of the most damaging arguments used against Breckinridge was that he was conspiring to destroy the Union. His enemies cited the support of William Lowndes Yancey of Alabama as prima facie evidence of this malicious intent. William T. Brown, district elector for Douglas, pictured the Alabama fire-eater as an archconspirator who for years had been "secretly waiting, watching, and plotting" the disruption of the Union. A. J. Keller of Raleigh told a meeting, "We must set ourselves firmly against the most unscrupulous men who ever threatened the welfare of the country." He warned against following the leadership of Yancey and Jefferson Davis. A Douglas ratification meeting in Pontotoc County, Mississippi, resolved: "That young Breckinridge of Kentucky in accepting the nomination of the bolters convention and uniting . . . with the desperate fortunes of Yancey and his followers, committed an act of folly which blights all his present fair prospects."[4]

In an effort to stamp out this insurgency, the Memphis supporters of Breckinridge called upon Yancey to come speak in Memphis to help combat the obstreperous Douglasites and the vociferous *Appeal*. The Alabaman enthusiastically agreed, because he too smarted from the stings of these attacks, which he said were "not urged through igno-

4. Memphis *Daily Appeal*, July 18, 21, 27, 1860.

rance or misapprehension, but as a part of a grand conspiracy entered into to destroy my character—in order to destroy to that extent the cause I advocate."[5]

To counter this strategy, Yancey recognized that he must answer the charges against his character and persuade the voters that he was not conspiring to destroy the Union. Furthermore, he realized that he must convince his Memphis listeners, who were firmly tied to the North and West, that the election of Breckinridge offered no threat to the Union.

A misunderstanding concerning the time of Yancey's arrival prevented the Breckinridge faction from staging an extravagant welcome. But in spite of "the shortness of the notice" a respectably large number of his friends met him on August 13 at the Memphis and Charleston station. When the famous Alabaman stepped from the train, he was greeted by "a salute of thirty guns," ushered into "an open barouche drawn by four beautiful horses," and escorted to the Gayoso House to the accompaniment of band music. That evening, preparatory to his appearance of the next day, the Breckinridge Association held a rally addressed by Captain James Hamilton and N. D. Collins. After the speaking, the members marched to the hotel, serenaded their famous guest, and cheered for a speech; but Yancey did not appear because, as the *Avalanche* explained, he was "too unwell."

Bellites and Douglas men, as well as Breckinridge supporters, poured into Memphis from all directions by foot, horseback, wagon, carriage, and railroad. A few came to clarify their thinking about confusing issues; some attended out of loyalty. Many, however, were pulled there by curiosity; they wanted to see and hear the famous fire-eater.

The great event was staged in the open space at the corner of Jefferson and Third streets. At 7:30 P.M. the cannon, near the speaker's stand, started booming. Bonfires were lighted, and "the

5. William L. Yancey to Beverly Matthews, August 6, 1860, in William L. Yancey Papers, Alabama State Department of Archives and History, Montgomery.

heavens were illuminated by the beautiful fireworks which were sent shooting up from the lot." By eight-thirty, spectators had filled "every vacant spot behind, in front and around the stand." The *Appeal* reported that the crowd was one of the largest "ever gathered together in the city."

The festivities opened with the Breckinridge and Lane clubs, led by "bands of music," parading through the streets and displaying numerous placards "beautifully painted" with appropriate mottoes. One eager young man carried a sign that read: WE WANT OUR RIGHTS—WE WILL HAVE THEM. PEACEABLY IF WE CAN—FORCIBLY IF WE MUST.

When Yancey mounted the platform at eight-thirty, his supporters gave him a great cheer, the cannon boomed again, and a last shower of rockets sprayed the sky. Flaming tar barrels and torches illuminated the area. An "experienced shorthand writer from Cincinnati," employed by the *Avalanche* especially "to take copy of speech," made last-minute preparations, and Yancey carefully arranged "his scrapbook and documents" on the speaking stand. The great moment was at hand.[6]

In opening, Yancey recognized that his greatest problem was one of personal vindication. He promised to speak "as one honest man ought to speak to another—frankly, truthfully, fearlessly" and to talk "in behalf of the Democracy, of the Constitution, and of Union under the Constitution."[7] He hoped to disarm his listeners immediately.

He reasoned that the best defense was a good offense; consequently, he devoted approximately 60 percent of his remarks to denouncing Stephen A. Douglas. Shifting attention away from himself, he accused Douglas of "designs to dismember" the Democracy, of plotting to defeat the two-thirds rule in the national Democratic convention at

6. Memphis *Avalanche*, August 14, 15, 1860.

7. The available text is probably not a verbatim report. Undoubtedly Yancey, or more likely M. W. Cluskey, editor of the *Avalanche*, edited the shorthand text to make it more readable. On the whole, however, the printed speech appears to be in oral style. The text is printed in full in the Memphis *Avalanche*, August 17, 1860.

Charleston, and of forcing the delegates to accept his views of the Kansas-Nebraska Act. "Mr. Douglas' friends forced us out of the Convention" and obtained their majority "by trickery," he said. This appeal was a strong emotional one. He defended his own part in the bolt: "Why did Yancey lead them? Did he pull the wool over their eyes? Had he seduced them? The [cotton] States left the national Democratic body . . . because its organization had fallen into the hands of men who thought more of the fortunes of Mr. Douglas than they did of the Constitution of their country or the Democracy." Yancey criticized the Baltimore convention for the seating of "bogus Democrats from Louisiana and Alabama"; he cast doubt on the legality of Douglas' nomination on the basis that he failed to receive a total vote equal to two-thirds of the number of electors in the electoral college; consequently, Yancey concluded that the Illinois senator stood "on the same footing as Breckinridge." Recognizing the weakness of this argument, the speaker hastened to show that Breckinridge deserved the Democratic votes because he was supported by the "truly Democratic States." He resorted to the bandwagon technique by suggesting that Breckinridge was endorsed by many prominent Democrats, including "every past living Democratic candidate for the presidency," the entire Buchanan cabinet, eight of the ten Democratic senators from the North, four-fifths of the Democratic representatives, every Democratic representative from Tennessee, and all the southern Democratic representatives and senators. Yancey then asked, "Will you put those broken-down politicians, Soule, Forsyth, Clemens, and your Footes against this mighty array of genius"?[8]

Yancey accused Douglas of "warring" on democracy in the past and cited as evidence his vote against the proslavery Lecompton constitution of Kansas and his advocacy of popular sovereignty. "Vengeance and Vengeance alone ought to be written as the motto on every Douglas banner that floats to the breeze," Yancey shouted.

8. Three of these were Douglas leaders: Pierre Soulé in Louisiana, John Forsyth in Alabama, and Henry S. Foote in Tennessee. Jere Clemens lived in Memphis and northern Alabama and supported Bell.

Before leaving the topic of the Illinois senator, Yancey attempted to stir the emotions of his Irish and German listeners by denouncing the recent efforts at fusion between Bellites and Douglasites in Kentucky. He shamed the Douglasites for plotting to join the American party, which four years before had campaigned on an anti-Catholic, anti-foreign platform. "Think of it, you Irish adopted citizens! Mark it well you Germans! Remember it you men who have thought that the American party were not for equal rights. Think of your being transferred like sheep and a 'bell' put on you. [Laughter and applause]."

After more than two hours, Yancey turned to an attack on John Bell and the Constitutional Unionists. Again he resorted to ridicule and stirred up strong emotions. "What is his record worth, honest men of Tennessee? The nominating Conventions won't declare his opinions, and he himself . . . won't declare his opinion—but he merely says 'I am for the Union, the Constitution, and the enforcement of the laws! . . .' And here, on this crisis in our country's destiny . . . John Bell and Edward Everett come before you with a padlock on their mouths and on their banners."

Yancey carefully avoided direct accusations of Bell but read to his tired audience several quotations from the *Congressional Globe* and various newspapers to support the frequently circulated charges that the Tennessean had favored abolition of slavery in the District of Columbia and had refused to support the Lecompton constitution. Yancey demonstrated that he considered Bell far less important than Douglas by devoting no more than 10 percent of his remarks to the Tennessean.

About midnight, following three hours of speaking, Yancey turned to direct defense of himself. A remark from the crowd, recorded in the *Avalanche's* account, suggests that some of his listeners had already departed. "You've got them down now. They are all leaving you." Yancey replied, "Oh, stay a little while longer. You abuse me three hundred and sixty-four days in the year! Give me one hour's chance—just one hour."

He dismissed as unfair and unimportant the accusations of disunionism leveled at him. In closing, he presented himself as an upright, patriotic southerner, whose only purpose was to defend southern rights.

> Oh! Gentlemen, how hard that he who is willing to forego office for years as I have done—asking nothing of the people, refusing the whole time since I was a young man to be connected in any way with candidacy for office, but the whole time giving my mind, intellect, heart, character, and money to try to raise the Southern mind to a perception of its rights, in order that we may be men in the hour that tries men's souls—how hard that such a man should be denounced as a demagogue, an office-seeker, and a traitor.

The *Avalanche* believed that Yancey had delivered a great oration. The editor of the Paris (Tennessee) *Patriot* reported, "We listened to his powerful oratory for four hours and like the thousands of others, of all parties, we sat entranced during the whole time." The *Morning Enquirer*, the Bell paper, said, "In some, perhaps in most respects, he met the expectations of those who attended, for he unquestionably has many of the qualities of an orator. . . . He was respectfully and attentively listened to, the large crowd doing credit to the character of Memphis for patience and orderly deportment." The *Daily Appeal* thought Yancey spoke "with caution. . . . There was some humor, a tolerable amount of sarcasm, and flashes of a driving impelling species of eloquence but as a whole there was heaviness in the argument."[9]

The newspapers reflected many of the attitudes of his auditors. Seemingly there was general agreement that Yancey was an eloquent speaker. The Breckinridge Democrats doubtlessly were entranced by the presentation of what they wanted to hear. The Bell and Douglas men, who went with closed minds, heard what they expected to hear; they were unmoved and perhaps more set in their opposition. On the other hand, the "orderly deportment" complimented Yancey. Three

9. For all of these responses to the speech, see Memphis *Daily Appeal*, August 15, 24, 1860.

days earlier, the Bell and Douglas supporters had completely broken up a meeting that Landon C. Haynes, state elector for Breckinridge, had attempted to address. Perhaps Edmund Ruffin's evaluation of another Yancey speech is applicable to this one. He said that Yancey was so fluent that he "did not know when to stop."[10]

Yancey minimized a direct discussion of the important issues and put his arguments in strong emotional terms. He sought to persuade Tennesseans to vote for Breckinridge because Bell and Douglas did not deserve their votes. Recognizing the widespread pro-Union attitudes, he wisely avoided discussing southern rights and secession, and concentrated upon a defense of his character, presenting himself as a staunch supporter of the Constitution and the Union. Well aware of the seriousness of the Douglas threat and the difficulty of converting old-time Whigs hardened by years of party discipline, he was equally wise to concentrate on Douglas instead of Bell.

Du Bose is probably correct in his belief that Yancey was eager to interpret "the national character of the Breckinridge campaign"; in addition to his immediate audience, the Alabaman probably hoped to reach a greater audience of Democrats throughout the Deep South and in the border and northern states. He wanted advance copy for his projected northern tour.[11]

From a long-range point of view, there is little to commend in Yancey's four-hour speech, which was little more than a vicious attack on Douglas and Bell based largely upon emotional appeal. Personal vindication was sound political strategy, but at a time when the country was on the threshold of civil war, this objective seems somewhat trivial. Whether Yancey did speak "frankly, truthfully, fearlessly" is doubtful.

In the next month, other important Breckinridge speakers des-

10. Memphis *Avalanche*, August 13, 1860; Avery O. Craven, *Edmund Ruffin, Southerner* (New York, 1930), 161.
11. John Witherspoon Du Bose, *The Life and Times of William Lowndes Yancey* (Birmingham, 1892), 490–91. The care taken to record the speech in shorthand

tined to play leading roles in the Confederacy spoke in Memphis. L. Q. C. Lamar, congressman from Mississippi, traveled across the state line to address an outdoor meeting on September 4. The newspapers failed to report his remarks, but they agreed that he was eloquent. While campaigning in northern Mississippi, Jefferson Davis stopped on September 22 to deliver a two-and-a-half-hour address in which he predicted that defeat of Breckinridge would mean dissolution of the Union. W. P. Miles of Louisiana and James R. Chalmers of Mississippi also appeared that night. Less than a week later, fresh from rallies at Shreveport, Louisiana, and Vicksburg, Mississippi, Louis T. Wigfall, fiery secessionist senator from Texas, spoke from the same platform. In spite of the prominence of these men, none received the attention given to Yancey. The speech of the Alabaman was reported in full and circulated in pamphlet form, but none of the others received so much as a column, even in the pro-Breckinridge *Avalanche*. Yancey's speech was considered a memorable event, but these later appearances were regarded as no more than interesting episodes.[12]

Today presidential electors play almost no part in a canvass, and the voters rarely know their names. But during the fall of 1860 the electors were extremely important; they traveled from place to place, debating usually for six or more hours every day. Each presented an opening speech from one to two hours long and, after his opponents' speeches, a thirty-minute rejoinder.

The electors of the Tenth Congressional District opened the Memphis series on August 20, and the subelectors of Shelby County

---

suggests this intention. M. W. Cluskey, who earlier had helped write the Breckinridge campaign literature and who was an editor of the *Avalanche*, was probably a great aid in planning this strategy and in circulating the speech in pamphlet form.

12. Memphis *Daily Appeal*, September 5, 19, 1860; Memphis *Avalanche*, September 5, 22, 24, 25, 28, 1860; Memphis *Enquirer*, September 23, 1860; Memphis *Argus*, September 24, 1860.

"divided time" on September 7. On September 11, three of the state electors—Landon C. Haynes for Breckinridge, William H. Polk, brother of the ex-president, for Douglas, and Balie Peyton for Bell—conducted a third debate.[13]

An incident during the third debate reflected the temper of the times. While on the platform, Polk was handed a written question asking whether the election of Lincoln would justify the breakup of the Union. Apparently avoiding an answer, Polk said to Haynes, "Stand up and tell these people your opinion of this question." When Haynes made no reply, the supporters of the Union shouted enthusiastically. During his rejoinder, Haynes dismissed the question as one written by an "old Federalist." Not liking the implication, W. D. Ferguson, the author, immediately denied the accusation. He asserted that he had fought in two wars, one under Andrew Jackson, and that he was prepared to fight again, if necessary, to prevent dissolution of the Union. Applause filled the hall. When the tumult subsided, Haynes countered that upon the first "overt act of aggression upon the rights of the South" he intended to ask Ferguson to accompany him to Washington to hang Lincoln. Haynes threatened to hang Ferguson "and all like him with grape vines" if he refused. The *Enquirer* reported that the interchange "created immense excitement." It indicated the growing frenzy gripping the South. Daily the press reported "multitudinous evidences of northern tampering with slaves," diabolical plots to burn towns, and the presence of mysterious strangers. Local groups organized to defend their homes in case Lincoln was elected.[14]

On October 6, the second set of state electors participated in the fourth debate, a five-hour verbal tussle that attracted a "rather slim"

13. Memphis *Avalanche*, August 18, 21, September 12, 1860; Memphis *Enquirer*, September 12, 1860; Memphis *Daily Appeal*, September 12, 1860.

14. Memphis *Enquirer*, September 12, 1860; Montgomery *Daily Mail*, August 16, 1860; Allan Nevins, *The Emergence of Lincoln* (2 vols.; New York, 1950), II, 306–309.

crowd. The newspapers attributed the poor attendance to the weather, but other signs indicated that the Memphis listeners were weary of the long campaign.[15]

During the first three months of the campaign, the Constitutional Unionists carried on their part of the debate through local groups and speakers. They seemed to feel outside help unnecessary. The split in the Democratic party gave them the comfortable feeling that they could win Tennessee.

But in September and October, the Bell and Everett men throughout the state were stirred to conduct a dramatic series of "protracted meetings." At Nashville on September 25, the citizens turned out in large numbers to hear John J. Crittenden and Horace Maynard. Crittenden was so delighted with the enthusiasm that he described the welcome extended him as befitting "twenty Presidents." At Knoxville, the bailiwick of Parson Brownlow, they held a two-day rally on September 27 and 28. Thousands came from all directions to participate in the festivities. Rival groups attempted to outdo each other in the parades; one delegation carried a persimmon tree covered with fruit and holding in its branches a live raccoon. The principal speakers were Benjamin H. Hill of Georgia, Leslie Coombs of Kentucky, and Horace Maynard. Brownlow reported, "It has been a successful, a glorious, and a terrible meeting. We use these words with emphasis."[16]

On October 8, the Memphis celebration, scheduled for a full week, opened while the Shelby County agricultural fair was in progress. The thousands reported present in holiday spirit were treated to a great parade of two thousand people, led by a wagon hauling a great bell, the symbol of the party. Close behind were carriages bearing William L. Sharkey, Thomas A. R. Nelson, and the other guests. A gaily

15. Memphis *Enquirer*, October 6, 1860; Memphis *Daily Appeal*, October 4, 5, 6, 1860; Memphis *Avalanche*, October 6, 1860.

16. Nashville *Banner*, September 25, 1860; Knoxville *Whig*, September 29, 1860; Parks, *John Bell*, 381–82.

decorated wagon, trimmed with red, white, and blue cloth, displayed twenty-seven young ladies, each representing a state and holding a sign bearing its name and emblem. Continuing the line of march were mounted citizens, two bands, and delegations from the states of Alabama, Louisiana, Mississippi, Kentucky, Illinois, Arkansas, and Missouri. The seven local Bell and Everett clubs brought up the rear.[17]

In the afternoon, Judge Sharkey of Mississippi spoke for three hours to an estimated 1,200 to 1,500 at Brinkley's Grove in northwest Memphis. He argued that the administration and the Democratic party were responsible for the difficulties of the time as well as for the agitation over slavery. Repeating a favorite Whig argument, he accused the Breckinridge wing of nominating its candidate for the purpose of assuring the election of Lincoln and thereby providing a spark to disrupt the Union. Since Lincoln and Breckinridge were sectional candidates and Douglas could not win, he contended, John Bell was the only man to "restore peace to the country." Sharkey concentrated his fire on Breckinridge and said little about Douglas. His speech was neither original in thought nor novel in expression.[18]

That night a second great rally was held at Court Square, "radiant with torches, lamps, and transparencies." After a torchlight procession, the crowd listened to Thomas A. R. Nelson and Andrew Jackson Donelson until well after midnight. The October 9 *Argus* reported this meeting to be "probably the largest political demonstration ever witnessed in Memphis." The following night Nathaniel G. Taylor, elector-at-large for Tennessee, addressed another rally, attended by four thousand to five thousand persons. Nelson talked to a third evening rally on October 10. He and several others had been drafted at the last moment because those scheduled could not appear. Expressing a sentiment commonly held, he declared that he did not consider the election of a "black Republican" sufficient cause to dis-

17. Memphis *Enquirer*, October 5, 9, 1860; Memphis *Daily Appeal*, October 9, 1860.
18. Memphis *Enquirer*, October 9, 1860.

rupt the Union and that he intended to resist aggression within the Union in the event of Lincoln's election.[19]

On Thursday evening Colonel Wood, state elector from Alabama, and John F. Sales of Memphis were pressed into service when the scheduled speakers again failed to appear. Even the *Enquirer* admitted a lack of enthusiasm but attributed it to the "cold and cheerlessness of the night." Probably the four nights of political polemics, combined with the county fair, nearly exhausted the Bell speakers and their supporters. The failure to hold previously announced meetings on Friday and Saturday, and the silence of the Whig *Enquirer* concerning the success of the Bellites, indicated that the "great national mass meeting" had, in the words of the *Avalanche*, "fizzled out."[20]

The rising tide of pro-Douglas sentiment in western Tennessee became a serious obstacle to the Breckinridge forces. They realized that a divided party had little chance of defeating an organization of old-time Whigs who habitually opposed Democrats, regardless of issues or personalities. On October 12, the Memphis *Avalanche* summarized their predicament. "Douglas, it is thought will not poll one thousand votes in Middle and East Tennessee. We assume that unless he polls six thousand votes in West Tennessee all is safe." But all was not safe in the Tenth Congressional District.

The Breckinridge Democrats needed a powerful voice to win votes away from Douglas. The *Avalanche* therefore announced with some satisfaction that "the old wheel horse, Andrew Johnson," had "taken the stump." In western Tennessee the senator had many friends, even among the Douglas faction, and was indeed welcome.[21] Disgruntled by the insurgency at Charleston and Baltimore, and suspicious of

19. Memphis *Argus*, October 9, 1860; Memphis *Daily Appeal*, October 9, 10, 1860; Memphis *Enquirer*, October 11, 12, 1860.
20. Memphis *Enquirer*, October 12, 1860; Memphis *Avalanche*, October 12, 1860.
21. Memphis *Avalanche*, October 9, 1860.

Yancey and the southern ultras, Johnson joined the campaign reluctantly, and only when he became fearful that John Bell, his bitter rival, might carry the state.

In the company of A. O. P. Nicholson, the other Tennessee senator, Johnson spoke on October 16 to what one paper termed a "very respectable audience." The *Avalanche*, after showing great enthusiasm over his coming, was strangely reticent in commenting on what he actually said. And there was a reason. The *Appeal*'s account provides an explanation for the terse report in the *Avalanche*. Johnson publicly denounced the bolts at Charleston and Baltimore, did not condemn Douglas to the nether region, and emphasized that he—refusing to follow the lead of Yancey—intended to fight for southern rights within the Union. Straddling the fence, he urged Tennesseans to vote for Breckinridge, but he suggested that in the northern states Democrats should vote for Douglas in order to defeat Lincoln. Consistent with his later actions, he dared to defy the extremists and refused to let the growing hysteria affect his thinking. The editor for the *Enquirer*, the Whig paper, wrote that in twenty-five years he had "never listened to an address so boiling over with rancorous venom," meaning, of course, that Johnson had viciously attacked John Bell. But this experience in western Tennessee convinced Johnson that a defeat was certain; consequently, he cut short his proposed tour and returned home discouraged, resigned to a Bell triumph.[22]

When he learned that the Pennsylvania Republicans had elected a governor, Douglas is reported to have said to his secretary, "Mr. Lincoln is the next President. We must try to save the Union. I will go South." For the second time in the campaign, the Illinois senator turned southward. On October 23, at Jackson, Tennessee, he addressed a gathering estimated at ten thousand for two and a quarter

22. Robert W. Winston, *Andrew Johnson, Plebeian and Patriot* (New York, 1928), 145–49; Memphis *Daily Appeal*, October 4, 17, 1860; Memphis *Avalanche*, October 20, 1860; Memphis *Enquirer*, October 18, 1860.

hours. En route to Memphis, he greeted crowds at Humboldt, Browns-ville, Mason's Depot, and Grand Junction, giving short speeches at two of these places.[23]

At eleven o'clock that night a huge delegation, including a local committee of fifty, forty marshals on horseback, seven Douglas clubs, and three bands, greeted him on his arrival in Memphis. His escort lifted him from the car and carried him to a waiting carriage. A second committee hurried Mrs. Douglas off by a private carriage away "from the arena of the hubbub and excitement." The newspapers reported that the bands played martial music and that skyrockets and Roman candles brightened the heavens. Soon the procession moved to the Gayoso House, where eager partisans blocked the main door, making it necessary for Douglas to slip in through the ladies' en-trance. A few minutes later Douglas appeared on the balcony, thanked his listeners for the "cordial reception," and begged to be excused because, as he explained, in the previous twenty-four hours he had made three speeches and had no sleep.[24]

On October 24, Memphis was filled with excited people, many of whom had come from as far away as Kentucky and Alabama. The Memphis and Charleston and the Mississippi and Tennessee railroads brought passengers to the city for half fare. A special train from Hernando, Mississippi, arrived in time for the speech.[25]

At 12:45 P.M. two bands, forty marshals, and hundreds of people on horseback escorted their hero to Market Square. The *Appeal* elo-quently reported, "Fair ladies and brave men stood along the side-walk, sending up incessant cheers, waving their handkerchiefs and bidding the honored guest . . . a happy 'God speed.'" Crowded into Market Square, leaving little room for those on foot, were carriages filled with ladies. Only after a half hour was sufficient area cleared to provide room for pedestrians. Eager listeners stood on the nearby

23. George Fort Milton, *The Eve of Conflict* (Boston, 1934), 496; Memphis *Daily Appeal*, October 23, 24, 25, 1860.
24. Memphis *Daily Appeal*, October 24, 1860.
25. *Ibid.*, October 25, 1860.

roofs and leaned out windows. Even the *Avalanche* estimated the crowd at five thousand.

In spite of a strenuous speaking schedule, Douglas was in good form; according to the *Appeal*, he could be heard at fifty yards, though his voice seemed harsher than usual.[26] Douglas came to quiet fears and stir loyalties; he came to reassure his listeners that they could live within the Union without fear of losing their property and that even the election of Lincoln was no cause for great alarm. He wanted to revitalize their patriotic sentiment and remind them of the common bonds existing between North and South.

In opening he emphasized, "I do not come to solicit your suffrage, but to make an appeal in behalf of this glorious Union by an exposition of those principles which in my opinion can only preserve the peace of this country." He devoted almost three-fourths of his speech to the "exposition" of the principles of popular sovereignty. "Can any man be a rational friend of his country who will not banish the whole subject from Congress, and let the people decide it, subject to the limitations of the Constitution?" asked Douglas.

In his own defense he became more direct and stated that he was advocating the same principles that he had fought for in 1856. Throughout his speech, he emphasized that southerners and northerners were equal under the law and that the federal government could not legally interfere with any domestic affair, including slavery. To answer the charge that he was conspiring with the Republicans, he turned the tables on the Breckinridge Democrats, accusing them of being responsible for Lincoln's successes: "Lincoln never had a ghost of a chance or a ray of hope of his election, without the aid of the Breckinridge men of the North."

Toward the end of his speech, the Illinoisan denounced disunion, expressing sentiments popular with many Tennesseans. "The election of no man on earth by the people, according to the Constitution is, of itself, justification for disunion. . . . We have already secured Demo-

26. *Ibid.*

cratic members of Congress, who, together with those elected in November, will hold the majority in connection with the South against the Black Republicans and prevent them from carrying out any improper designs." He thought that secession provided no remedy for the problems facing the country. To the contrary, he said, "the one mode of preserving" the Union was "by maintaining, inviolate, every duty imposed by it." He reasserted, "I am for maintaining this, a government of laws, in opposition to mob violence and lynch law, and disunion and secession."

The undertone of this talk was a defense of his own character. Like Yancey, Douglas felt that he must defend his conduct; consequently, he sought to show that he was acting honorably, was consistent, and was moved by worthy motives.

In some respects the speech is significant for what Douglas did not say. At no time did he ask for support at the polls; he never indicated what he might or might not do if elected. He referred neither to Bell nor the Constitutional Union party. He cast no aspersions on the character of Lincoln. He completely ignored Yancey, making no mention of his northern tour, then in progress. He directed his attacks mainly at Breckinridge and Jefferson Davis.

This two-and-a-half-hour address, with its detailed interpretation of popular sovereignty, fell short of being a great, stirring appeal to save the Union. Seemingly it lacked fire and inspiration. The noble intentions of Douglas cannot be denied, but the execution of those intentions missed the mark.

Many persons of Memphis must have been near exhaustion when election day finally came on November 6, 1860. One or two political meetings had been held almost every weekday night for four months. Hundreds of speeches had been delivered. The quantity of gunpowder used to fire salutes was enormous. Hardly a week passed without at least one parade. At moments when the local scene became dull, there were always barbecues and rallies in nearby counties to attend. No record exists concerning the amount of liquor consumed in toasting the respective candidates, a typical custom of the day, but it is likely that, if Memphis was like other river towns, the 125 saloons poured out barrels in the cause of conviviality. Furthermore, no record is extant of the fistfights that must have ensued when words became inadequate. Nevertheless, the newspapers' reports are sufficient to indicate the intensity of the campaign.

Bell carried Tennessee, winning 69,710 votes; Breckinridge polled 65,053; and Douglas, a poor third, received only 11,384. Bell showed his greatest strength in eastern Tennessee, Breckinridge was strongest in middle Tennessee, and Douglas won most of his votes in the southwestern counties near Memphis. Bell's victory represented strictly a Whig vote, varying little from the Whig vote of the previous twenty years. He probably won because the Democratic vote was split between his two opponents.[27]

In the Tenth Congressional District, Bell likewise led with 7,094 votes, but contrary to the trend in the state as a whole, Douglas was second with 5,183 votes while Breckinridge polled only 2,481. In only one of the five counties did Breckinridge top Douglas, and then by a plurality of only 31 votes. Nearby Tipton County, just north of Shelby but in another congressional district, gave Douglas more votes than either of his opponents, and the city of Memphis also put Douglas first.[28]

In many ways, the outcome of the election in the Tenth Congressional District represented a real triumph for the Douglas Democrats, for more than twice as many persons in southwestern Tennessee preferred Douglas to Breckinridge. In contrast to the situation in neighboring states, loyalties to Douglas and his cause were maintained, and a state organization remained in the field even though opposition seemed futile. Furthermore, the Douglas vote in the

---

27. Memphis *Avalanche*, October 25, 1860; Memphis *Daily Appeal*, October 25, 1860; Marguerite Bartlett Hamer, "The Presidential Campaign of 1860 in Tennessee," *East Tennessee Historical Society Publications*, No. 3 (1931), 3–22; Thomas Perkins Abernethy, *From Frontier to Plantation in Tennessee* (Chapel Hill, 1932), 336.

28. *Tribune Almanac: 1861* (New York, 1862), 54.

Tenth Congressional District was sufficient to spell defeat for Breckinridge and the secessionists in Tennessee and to throw the election to Bell, whose plurality was less than five thousand votes. A positive expression of pro-Union sympathy was probably Douglas' real objective, regardless of whether the votes were cast for him or for Bell. Douglas and his followers took satisfaction in the belief that, for the moment, they had foiled the conspiracy of the extremists to bring about a coup d'etat and to sweep the entire South into immediate secession.[29]

Obviously, many factors accounted for the outcome of the election in southwestern Tennessee. First, traditional ties among old-time Whigs were strong enough to assure the Constitutional Unionists a vote large enough to defeat a divided Democratic party. Second, the strong local Douglas organization, the efforts of the Memphis *Appeal*, and Douglas' speeches in western Tennessee prevented complete annihilation of the Douglas wing. Third, Yancey and the "bolters" seemingly could find no arguments at the moment strong enough to win over those Memphis business interests who saw in secession a threat to their prosperity. Fourth, the Breckinridge forces were probably ineffective in gaining the support of the foreign-born—the Irish and Germans—and this group naturally preferred Douglas to Bell, who was tainted with Know-Nothingism. Fifth, the frenzy that was sweeping the lower South had not gained sufficient momentum in Memphis by election time to influence the vote.

But the pro-Union victory in Tennessee was a hollow one. Once the election was over, the pro-Union forces relaxed, and the secessionist forces redoubled their efforts. Within a year Tennessee was caught up in the onrushing tide of secession. Political figures who had supported Bell and Douglas, perhaps somewhat awed by the growing strength of secessionist feeling, joined in the movement to split the Union asunder.

29. Percy Lee Rainwater, *Mississippi: Storm Center of Secession* (Baton Rouge, 1938), 135–60, 198–99; Nevins, *The Emergence of Lincoln*, II, 293–95.

···✦✦[IV]✦✦···
Myths in
a Rhetorical Context

In 1894, when Senator Matt W. Ransom of North Carolina appeared headed for defeat at the hands of the Populists, a fellow politician recommended to the senator a popular strategy to overcome his difficulty. He suggested "getting Genl [John B.] Gordon to deliver his lecture on 'the last days of the Confederacy,' inviting the country people, and getting him to make an allusion to you." It was rumored that Gordon worked great magic when telling his tales of the Lost Cause and the Old South and was effective in casting favor on anyone he endorsed and in destroying those he opposed. On one occasion the Nashville *Banner* reported, "As he [Gordon] described scene after scene his audience wept with him, listened breathlessly lest they should lose a word." In his oft-repeated lecture, Gordon revived memories of halcyon antebellum days and exciting moments of the late war and fascinated listeners with romantic and heroic accounts of bravery, compassion, and patriotism. Perhaps one writer was not exaggerating when he called Gordon's eloquence entrancing. Gordon, commander-in-chief of the United Confederate Veterans from 1890 to 1904 and the very personification of the southern gentleman and the Confederate hero, was well-practiced in exploiting the myths of the South for political purposes and for profit. Like many southern politicians, he turned frequently to the power of mythology.[1]

1. R. J. Brevard to M. W. Ransom, July 3, 1894, quoted in C. Vann Woodward, *Origins of the New South, 1877–1913* (Baton Rouge, 1951), 158; Nashville

Another artist at using myth as an effective persuasive device was Henry W. Grady. Into many of his speeches the Atlanta editor worked the four most popular southern myths: the Old South, the Lost Cause, the Solid South, and the New South. He once told an Augusta, Georgia, audience:

> Had *Uncle Tom's Cabin* portrayed the habit rather than the exception of slavery, the return of the Confederate armies could not have stayed the horrors of arson and murder their departure would have invited. Instead of that, witness the miracle of the slave in loyalty closing the fetters about his own limbs—maintaining the families of those who fought against his freedom—and at night on the far-off battlefield searching among the carnage for his young master, that he might lift the dying head to his tender breast and with rough hands wipe the blood away, and bend his tender ear to catch the last words for the old ones at home, wrestling meanwhile in agony and love, that in vicarious sacrifice he would have laid down his life in his master's stead. This friendliness, thank God, has survived the lapse of years, the interruption of factions, and the violence of campaigns, in which the bayonet fortified, the drumbeat inspired. Though unsuspected in slavery, it explains the miracle of '64—though not yet confessed, it must explain the miracle of 1888.[2]

Into these four sentences Grady wove at least ten appeals to the major myths. He summoned memories of the Old South by his references to *Uncle Tom's Cabin*, the loyalty of slaves to the family, the slave's tenderness to his dying "young master," and the "friendliness" between the races that "survived." But interspersed in the passage are references to the Lost Cause—"the Confederate armies," "the far-off battlefield," "the carnage," and "vicarious sacrifice." Into the last sentence Grady inserted a veiled reference to the New South ("the

---

Banner, June 25, 1896; Howard Dorgan, "A Case Study in Reconciliation: General John B. Gordon and 'The Last Days of the Confederacy,'" *Quarterly Journal of Speech*, LX (1974), 83–91.

2. From a speech delivered in November, 1887, at the Augusta Exposition, reprinted in *The New South: Writings and Speeches of Henry Grady* (Savannah, 1971), 54.

miracle of 1888"). The total context clearly evoked the myth of the Solid South to those present. Attuned to the attitudes of fellow southerners, Grady knew that these references had emotional pull and that his listeners could not resist romantic visions of plantation days and the intense hatred for the enemy in the late war. He knew also that such "snake oil" was entrancing.

After the Civil War, southern speakers repeatedly made use of myths in their ceremonial oratory to reconcile southerners to defeat and rebuild their self-esteem.[3] But how did these myths gain such power over southerners? What was their rhetorical significance? What is the nature of the social myth and how does its persuasion work in oral discourse?

The word *myth* is not an easy term to define or even explain, because it is elusive and nebulous and depends for its force upon its loose structure. It has become a means of dramatizing deep-seated group yearnings and values. One authority suggests, "No human society has yet been found in which such mythological motifs have not been rehearsed in liturgies; interpreted by seers, poets, theologians, or philosophers; presented in art; magnified in song; and ecstatically experienced in life-empowering visions."[4]

Leo Marx thinks that myth "is difficult to define or even locate because it is an expression less of thought than of feeling. . . . It is widely diffused in our culture, insinuating itself into many kinds of behavior." According to Walter Lippmann, "The distinguishing mark of a myth is that truth and error, fact and fable, report and fantasy are all on the same plane of credibility. . . . What a myth never contains is the critical power to separate its truth from its error." Henry Nash Smith labels the myth "an intellectual construction that

3. I have discussed these myths at length in "Repining over an Irrevocable Past: The Ceremonial Orator in a Defeated Society, 1865–1900," in *Oratory in the New South*, ed. Waldo W. Braden (Baton Rouge, 1979), 8–37.

4. Joseph Campbell, "The Historical Development of Mythology," in *Myth and Mythmaking*, ed. Henry A. Murray (Boston, 1960), 19.

fuses concept and emotion into an image. . . . [Myths are] collective representations rather than the work of a single mind." Marx agrees that as a "cultural symbol," myth is the "product of the collective imagination." Calling it "a collective affair," R. W. B. Lewis says, "It must be pieced together out of an assortment of essays, orations, poems, stories, histories, and sermons."[5]

These sources suggest that the myth draws upon memory and imagination; that it results from a collective effort over a considerable period of time; that it represents an oversimplification of events, persons, and relationships; that it is more emotional than logical in its substance; and that it combines both reality and fiction. In other words, it is the product of considerable abstracting on the part of many people.[6]

Intellectual and social historians have spent considerable time seeking out the influence of myth as it appears in all types of discourse, but they have given their main attention to the written rather than the spoken. In a significant book entitled *Virgin Land: The American West as Symbol and Myth*, Henry Nash Smith "traces the impact of the West, the vacant continent beyond the frontier, on the consciousness of Americans and follows the principal consequences of this impact in literature and social thought."[7] He finds the myth of the West in the writings of Thomas Jefferson, Thomas Hart Benton, William Gilpin,

5. Leo Marx, *The Machine in the Garden: Technology and the Pastoral Ideal in America* (New York, 1964), 4–5; Walter Lippmann, *Public Opinion* (New York, 1932), 123; Henry Nash Smith, *Virgin Land: The American West as Symbol and Myth* (Cambridge, 1950), vii; R. W. B. Lewis, *The American Adam: Innocence, Tragedy and Tradition in the Nineteenth Century* (Chicago, 1955), 4.

6. In formulating my ideas about myth and in gathering materials for this paper, I am indebted to many of my students who participated in my seminars on southern oratory. The studies of two of my former students have provided me valuable insight into the subject. See Howard Dorgan, "Southern Apologetic Themes as Expressed in Selected Ceremonial Speaking of Confederate Veterans, 1889–1900" (Ph.D. dissertation, Louisiana State University, 1971), and Raymond Buchanan, "The Epideictic Speaking of Robert Love Taylor Between 1891 and 1906" (Ph.D. dissertation, Louisiana State University, 1970).

7. Smith, *Virgin Land*, 4.

and Asa Whitney, who portrayed the West as the "highway to the Pacific, the passage to India, the manifest destiny" of the United States, the garden of the world, and the frontier. He sees the evolving legend of the West expressed in fictional characters such as Daniel Boone, Leatherstocking, the mountain man, Kit Carson, Buffalo Bill, Deadwood Dick, and Calamity Jane.

Having the advantage of Smith's insights, Marx has produced an equally revealing study, *The Machine in the Garden*. Searching through many types of American writings, he notes the influences of "the pastoral ideal" upon those who have "the yearning for a simpler, more harmonious style of life, an existence closer to nature." He finds expressions of this theme in the writing of Nathaniel Hawthorne, Henry David Thoreau, Ralph Waldo Emerson, Walt Whitman, and others.[8]

Richard Hofstadter, the historian, interprets nineteenth-century America in terms of the agrarian myth. He argues that myth implies an "idea . . . that so effectively embodies men's values that it profoundly influences their ways of perceiving reality and hence their behavior. In this sense, myths may have varying degrees of fiction or reality." He shows that "the agrarian myth was first the notion of the educated classes, of those who enjoyed a classical education, read pastoral poetry . . . and owned plantations or country estates." He suggests its nature and complexities in his discussion of the "component themes" of the agrarian myth.

> Like any complex of ideas, the agrarian myth cannot be defined in a phrase, but its component themes form a clear pattern. Its hero was the yeoman farmer, its central conception the notion that he is the ideal man and the ideal citizen. Unstinted praise of the special virtues of the farmer and the special values of rural life was coupled with the assertion that agriculture, as a calling uniquely productive and uniquely important to society, had a special right to the concern and protection of government. The yeoman, who owned a small farm and worked it with

8. Marx, *The Machine in the Garden*.

the aid of his family, was the incarnation of the simple, honest, independent, healthy, happy human being. Because he lived in close communion with the beneficent nature, his life was believed to have a wholesomeness and integrity impossible for the depraved populations of cities. His well-being was not merely physical, it was moral; it was not merely personal, it was the central source of civic virtue; it was not merely secular but religious, for God had made the land and called man to cultivate it. Since the yeoman was believed to be both happy and honest, and since he had a secure propertied stake in society in the form of his own land, he was held to be the best and most reliable sort of citizen.[9]

In this explanation, Hofstadter demonstrates another characteristic of myth—its association with positive words. The following words are illustrative: ideal, productive, simple, honest, independent, healthy, happy, wholesome, moral, best, reliable.

The parallel between the agrarian myth and the four southern myths is striking. Orators, journalists, and novelists had much to do with formulating and popularizing these southern myths. William Taylor shows that the romanticized South appeared in novels long before the Civil War.[10] The Old South image, growing rapidly after Appomattox, embraced a kaleidoscopic composite of plantation life, a romantic fantasy dear to southerners: the white-columned mansion, acres of snowy cotton, the coquettish belle, the genteel master, the crooning mammy, singing field hands, reckless young gallants, and a native chivalry.

In a single paragraph, General Gordon could express many of these romantic dimensions. "No age or country has ever produced a civilization of a nobler type than that which was born in the southern plantation home. . . . It was a civilization where personal courage, personal independence, personal dignity, personal honor, and the

---

9. Richard Hofstadter, *The Age of Reform: From Bryan to FDR* (New York, 1981), 24–25.
10. William R. Taylor, *Cavalier and Yankee: The Old South and American National Character* (London, 1963), 145–76.

manliest virtues were nurtured; where feminine refinement, feminine
culture, delicacy, and gentleness expressed themselves in models of
rarest loveliness and perfection; and where, in the language of a great
Georgian, hospitality was as free and boundless as the vitalizing air
around us." [11]

The novel and movie *Gone With the Wind* dramatized these same
elements. The myth comes to life in the persons of Scarlet O'Hara,
Rhett Butler, and Ashley Wilkes, in the destruction of the plantation
Tara, the conflagration of the war, the horrors of Reconstruction, and
the demise of the old way of life. Of course, *The Birth of a Nation*,
adapted from Thomas Dixon's novel *The Clansman*, was an equally
successful exploiter of the Lost Cause. The configuration of these
elements in speeches, novels, and films formed a vision of an idealized
romantic style of life that never existed, but one that provided a
retreat from sober reality. Woodrow Wilson summarized the effects of
these persuasive efforts in his comment about *The Birth of a Nation*,
which he said was like "writing history with lightning." [12]

Only after the Civil War and Reconstruction did southerners as a
whole embrace this fanciful vision of the antebellum South. Prior to
1860 many were more likely to think of themselves as Virginians,
Mississippians, or Georgians; persons on different economic levels
had diverse goals. But after 1865 large numbers sought to trace their
lineage to great plantation families and prided themselves on being
southerners.

The modern advertiser has learned the advantages that accrue by
relating his product to the legends of the West and the South. Americans from the time of Jamestown have been enamored with the allure
of the frontier and the West. When Horace Greeley advised, "Go
West, young man," he was broadcasting on this wavelength. Recently an arms manufacturer appealed to the western myth in an

11. John B. Gordon, *The Old South* (Augusta, Ga., 1887), 7–8. This pamphlet is
the printed version of an address delivered on Confederate Memorial Day, 1887, at
the ninth reunion of the Confederate Survivors' Association of Augusta.

12. Jack Temple Kirby, *Media-Made Dixie* (Baton Rouge, 1978), 4.

advertisement: "Wrap your hand around the grips and put yourself right back through history when Colt's fabled Single Acting Army became man's constant companion on the trail and by lonely campsites. You'll feel the same confidence, the same pride of possession as did these early pioneers." John Barnett of the *Wall Street Journal*, spotting the appeal of the passage, said: "Colt's advertising copywriters have zeroed in on a salient fact: Many Americans have never outgrown the frontier." The fantasy of cowboys and Indians has become a worldwide craze that demands broad sombreros, leather chaps, jingling spurs, faded blue jeans, holstered six-guns, and crude tomahawks.[13]

It is equally true that the southern myths retain tremendous appeal. Advertisers know that the great plantation home, with manly southern gentlemen and ladies in hoopskirts in front of its elegant entrance, lends sophistication to a product, particularly to whiskeys. A Kentucky colonel, stereotyped by his beard and dress, sells Kentucky fried chicken. The University of Mississippi football team, known as "the Rebels," is squired about by a stereotyped southern gentleman, accompanied by a marching band dressed in Confederate uniforms, with one of their number waving the Stars and Bars. The playing of "Dixie" is still a sure way to arouse great outbursts of southern patriotism and bring favor to anyone who is capable of giving a healthy Rebel yell.

The various studies cited earlier suggest the unfolding elements of the social myth. When people find their immediate situations unpleasant and unsatisfying, they seek escape to a simpler existence. Hence our forefathers, who encountered religious and political persecution in Europe, sought the New World, where they dreamed of building a heaven on earth, a theocracy based upon God's law, free from the restrictions of the established church and beyond the reach of

13. *Wall Street Journal*, June 9, 1972. See also Ray A. Billington, "Cowboys, Indians, and the Land of Promise: The World Image of the American Frontier," in *Representative American Speeches, 1975–1976*, ed. Waldo W. Braden (New York, 1976), 176–98.

the English courts. Early inhabitants living near the Atlantic sea-board looked longingly across the Alleghenies for cheap land. In story and movie, Daniel Boone became the personification of the brave, heroic frontiersman pushing beyond the villages taking shape to the wilderness, where he would escape the restrictions of civilization.[14] Seeing their old ways destroyed by war and Reconstruction, southern-ers retreated to a mythical Old South or took succor in the santifica-tion of the defeat of the Confederacy, comparing it to Christ's crucifix-ion. Today, Americans living in cities rebel against overcrowding and seek solace in the suburbs or the country, away from machines, traffic, and smog. It appears that unhappy people pine for simpler, idealized, romantic places: a Garden of Eden, a Valhalla, an Arcadia, a rustic cabin, or even "a little gray home in the West."

The focus of this essay is upon myth as it is used in oral persuasion, and not upon its more refined versions as they appear in the novels of William Faulkner and the plays of Tennessee Williams. Differentiat-ing between the two types, Marx characterizes the first as "popular and sentimental" and the second as "imaginative and complex."[15] Of course, the two are seldom mutually exclusive, but keeping in mind the distinction between them is important. In the hands of a skillful writer, a myth becomes subtle, refined, and even poetic, eliciting the resources of memory and imagination. But a myth presented by a popular orator may become bold, crass, and vulgar. When it is re-ported and transcribed after the fact, it may appear blatant and even ridiculous. Dismissing it, a critical reader may ask, "How could the audience be taken in by such shoddy means?" But at the moment of utterance in the speeches of a Vardaman, Bilbo, Watson, Tillman, Wallace, or Maddox, the myth is highly moving, particularly before rural audiences conditioned by its frequent repetition. And there is no denying that certain myths have demonstrated their continued attrac-tiveness for over a hundred years and have kept alive cultural isolation

14. Smith, *Virgin Land,* 1–59.
15. Marx, *The Machine in the Garden,* 5.

and even racial hatred in the South. Sometimes vicious and venal, they have quieted debate, driven out opposition, and stifled needed reform.

Kenneth Burke explains persuasion in terms of identification, or of the speaker's becoming "substantially one" with his listeners. In clarifying his meaning, Burke employs a good theological term—*consubstantiality*—meaning the development of "common sensations, concepts, images, ideas, attitudes" between persons who identify with each other. Burke continues: "As for the relation between 'identification' and 'persuasion': we might well keep it in mind that a speaker persuades an audience by the use of stylistic identifications; his act of persuasion may be for the purpose of causing the audience to identify itself with the speaker's interests; and the speaker draws on identification of interests to establish rapport between himself and his audience. So, there is no chance of our keeping apart the meaning of persuasion, identification ('consubstantiality') and communication (the nature of rhetoric as 'addressed')." [16]

The myth provides a potent means of establishing identification, or consubstantiality. When the speaker activates the myth, listeners feel kinship or oneness with him. Setting imaginations in motion, he stirs up many associations. A single sign may stimulate a variety of emotional responses and draw from unexpressed longings. The listener forgets present complexities and fantasizes a simplistic vision, often calming, romantic, and dreamlike. Fantasy sometimes completely replaces reality. When the identification is strong, the speaker may produce something near mass hypnotism, gaining the power to make his slightest suggestion a command to the faithful. This is the stuff that leaders like Hitler or certain evangelists use to exploit and mesmerize their followers. Hence, when mobs lose control of their rational judgment, they respond to appeals of a vicious kind that may result in great harm.

The possibility of consubstantiality explains why myth presents

16. Kenneth Burke, *A Rhetoric of Motives* (New York, 1953), 21, 46.

the rhetorical critic with difficulty. Since the members of an audience may possess a myth in common and even revere it, the orator or writer who uses the myth seldom needs to present it in a full-blown form; instead he suggests or insinuates it through signs, phrases, allusions, passing references, or gestures. A physical symbol may heighten consubstantiality. For example, the presence of John B. Gordon, Jefferson Davis, or Robert E. Lee once revived memories of the Lost Cause. A battle flag, a Confederate uniform, and an armless sleeve were equally stirring signs of the Lost Cause. What the reader finds in the printed version of a speech might be only a small part of the myth, the tiny hint of what grinds inside frustrated listeners. Sometimes the trigger for the myth does not even appear in the printed version, because face-to-face the listeners and speaker, feeling a oneness, evoke the myth without verbal expressions.

A basic requirement for continued existence of a myth is that it be accepted without reflection or questioning. Drawing upon imagination, it strives to elicit what is pleasant, soothing, and satisfying, and gains acceptance and strength through repetition. Hofstadter concludes that "the agrarian myth came to be believed more widely and tenaciously as it became more fictional."[17]

Obviously, the main function of myth is to confirm, intensify, and amplify existing sentiments and attitudes. It acts upon beliefs already possessed. For those who cannot or do not wish to face reality, it provides rationalizations, escapes, and fantasy. In many instances, the myth is like a blank form onto which the listener may fill in any meaning, feeling, or longing that he abstracts from what is pleasant while he ignores or forgets what is disturbing. Speaking of these tendencies among southerners after the Civil War, T. Harry Williams concludes, "This cherishing of an ideal dream world in the past was both a reflection of the Southerner's capacity for unreality and a cause of his continuing reluctance to face the realities of the modern world;

17. Hofstadter, *The Age of Reform*, 30.

for obviously the myth of a perfect society was a powerful argument against change, against even considering whether there was any need for change." [18]

Membership in the group often depends upon continued overt demonstration of faithful acceptance of various facets of the imaginary picture. Furthermore, the possessors and believers jealously guard the integrity of the myth and permit no challenge to it. To be suspected of being a nonbeliever or doubter may result in one's being ostracized. The faithful resort to name-calling and the strategy of terror to quiet or embarrass anyone who shows independence. Concerning the myth builders in the South, for example, Henry Savage, Jr., observes: "Once the glorified and purified conceptions of the old South as a golden age without shadows and the Confederacy as all dash, gallantry, and sacrifice were embraced, they were enshrined in Southerner's hearts. In effect, Southerners had made a religion of the old South and the Confederacy, replete with unchallengeable tenets, ritual, hallowed saints, and sacred shrines. Any criticism, even any factual derogation of those enshrined concepts came to be regarded as blasphemy." [19]

In the postbellum South, those who did not embrace the myth were castigated as carpetbaggers, scalawags, nigger-lovers, and Yankees. In the 1960s, orators called integrationists and those who favored abiding by federal court decisions Communists, left-wingers, subversives, agitators, fanatics, and atheists. Perhaps this climate explains why young intellectuals such as Walter Hines Page and many who followed him found it desirable to leave their native states for more congenial companionship outside Dixie.

The typical ceremonial speech provides an excellent vehicle for utilizing the myth. Before he takes the platform, the panegyrist knows that

18. T. Harry Williams, *Romance and Realism in Southern Politics* (Athens, Ga., 1961), 7.
19. Henry Savage, Jr., *Seeds of Time* (New York, 1959), 198.

his listeners are in harmony with his point of view, the occasion, and other audience members, that they are not eager to have their opinions and beliefs disturbed, and that they have assembled for emotional support and inspiration. Consequently, ideas do not need to be proved or supported by facts and authority; they need only to be magnified. In this atmosphere, the speaker finds that how he expresses his message becomes more important than what the message is. He may clothe his message in what the ancient critics called the grand style. In this case he would tend toward language that is ornate, figurative, euphonious, and polished, and would become rotund in voice and sweeping in his total manner. Quite possibly it is from using this mode that the southern speaker has gained his reputation for grandiloquent style and impassioned delivery.

General Gordon, one of the most popular post–Civil War lecturers and patriotic orators in both North and South, was a mythmaker of a high order. To maintain his popularity, the old general adeptly walked a narrow line, stirring southern emotions without offending Yankee sentiments. He kept a full schedule of lectures and supported himself by his lecture fees. As an expert practitioner of the rhetoric of accommodation, he filled his talks with appeals to popular myths. He demonstrated his skill in his address to a meeting of Confederate veterans in 1887 in Augusta, Georgia, where his appeals to the Lost Cause, the New South, and a southern patriotic fervor were most welcome. The following passage will serve to illustrate Gordon's technique.

> And after the war, with her substance wasted, her hopes blasted and her soil still wet with the blood of her sons, even then, turning her grief-furrowed face to the God whom she had served, and without a murmur upon her lips, she cried in mingled agony of faith struggling with despair: "Though He slay me, yet will I trust in him."
>
> . . . The new and robust life upon which, through the ashes and ravages of war, the South has already entered, inspires our hearts with the most buoyant hopes of the future. Knee deep in these ruins, she has waded through them for a decade and erect in her conscious power, she

challenged the confidence and invited the co-operation and capital of other sections; and she furnishes to-day a field for richer returns—more certain profits than any portion of our country. Her doors are thrown wide open and her heart's welcome is given to all who may find homes in her hospitable climate. Her future wealth seems assured. In another decade the roar of her great forges, the thunder of her water powers, driving her millions of spindles, will prove the century's marvel of industrial progress. But while we press to their utmost the practicable development of our admitted agricultural advantages and give encouragement to the spirit of enterprise manifested on every hand, we must permit no decrease of interest in the political welfare of the whole country. Wedded inseparably to the constitutional rights of the States, let us cultivate, by all legitimate means, a broad nationality embracing the whole union of States. Here hangs above us the flag of that union. Let us honor it as the emblem of freedom, of equality, and unity— remembering that there is not a star on its blue field which is not made brighter by light reflected from southern skies—not a white line in its folds but what is made whiter and purer by the South's incorruptible record—not one of its crimson stripes that is not deeper and richer from southern blood shed in its defense in all of the wars with foreign powers.[20]

These two paragraphs taken from the heart of the address provide an excellent example of how, as a conciliator, Gordon, himself a great symbol of the Lost Cause, appealed to ardent ex-Confederates, some perhaps in faded uniforms and still embittered by defeat, to move beyond bitterness and remorse toward a future as loyal Americans. He reached the climax of his rhetorical strategy when he asked his listeners to honor the flag "as the emblem of freedom, of equality and unity." His skill in rhetorical maneuver is best shown in this rhetoric of accommodation, which provides succor for both Yankees and Confederates and for both past and future.

How does the myth work in a deliberative speech that advocates a change of policy requiring proof? How can a myth be made support-

20. Gordon, *The Old South*, 12.

ive of, or a substitute for, argument and evidence? Obviously, it is not appropriate for the speaker who faces questions, demands for facts, close reasoning, and verifiable sources. When he enjoys a good reputation and high credibility (ethos), the advocate may use the myth in the same way he does in the ceremonial speech. In this instance the speaker needs to amplify his argument and relate it to listeners' needs and wants. Drawing upon imagination, he may enhance pathetic appeals and expand, intensify, and emotionalize the point under consideration. In his "Cross of Gold" speech, William Jennings Bryan bolstered an argument by alluding to a myth. "You come to us and tell us that the great cities are in favor of the gold standard; we reply that the great cities rest upon our broad and fertile prairies. Burn down your cities and leave our farms, and your cities will spring up again as if by magic; but destroy our farms and the grass will grow in the streets of every city in the country." [21] Bryan knew that his opponents could not risk denying a commonly accepted belief concerning the importance of agriculture in the national development and that in spite of the growing industrialism in the last half of the nineteenth century, Americans felt kinship with, and associated their prosperity with, the yeoman farmer.

John C. Calhoun, in his famous speech of March 4, 1850, delivered in the United States Senate, made telling use of the myth of George Washington in a deliberative context. To understand Calhoun's rhetorical tack, the reader must remember that by 1850, the Father of His Country was used frequently as a symbol to stir loyalty and patriotism. "At the mere mention of The Patriot Father's 'magic name,'" declared Governor Henry A. Wise, "Civil Discord hushes into awed silence, schisms and sections are subdued and vanish; for in the very naming of that name, there is . . . the spell of Order, and Liberty, and Law, and the strength and beauty of *National* Union." [22] Therefore, to imply Washington's endorsement was high persuasion.

21. A. Craig Baird, *American Public Address, 1740–1952* (New York, 1956), 199.

22. Quoted in Bernard Mayo, *Myths and Men* (Athens, Ga., 1959), 25.

In this instance the South Carolinian turned the tables on his northern listeners in his explanation of how the Union could not be saved.

Nor can the Union be saved by invoking the name of the illustrious Southerner whose mortal remains repose on the western bank of the Potomac. He was one of us—a slave holder and a planter. We have studied his history, and find nothing in it to justify submission to wrong. On the contrary, his great fame rests on the solid foundation, that while he was careful to avoid doing wrong to others, he was prompt and decided in repelling wrong. I trust that, in this respect, we profited by his example.

Nor can we find anything in his history to deter us from seceding from the Union, should it fail to fulfill the objects for which it was instituted, by being permanently and hopelessly converted into the means of oppression instead of protection. On the contrary, we find much in his example to encourage us, should we be forced to the extremity of deciding between submission and disunion.[23]

Calhoun's rhetoric, reminiscent of Patrick Henry's, was moving, because it drew its strength from the symbolism of the American Revolution and took full possession of the Washington myth.

The previous discussion suggests several characteristics of the myth as a persuasive device. First, a myth has a complex structure that seldom remains fixed or constant. Its implications and influence shift from occasion to occasion, from speaker to speaker, and from speech to speech. Its coloring is affected by local customs and preferences, emotional conditioning, and the degree of intensity with which it is believed.

A myth draws together various themes, and it often intertwines itself with related concepts. These threads may not be consistent or orderly. The speakers must keep these antagonistic feelings rationalized for the listeners. For example, a southern speaker may at one moment commend the happy slave on the old plantation and in the

23. Baird, *American Public Address*, 83.

next instance denounce the black as a threat to white supremacy. Grady and Gordon praised the Old South, yet advocated the New South. Although the goals of the two Souths were different, these persuaders cleverly construed one to be the extension of the other.

Second, the myth is established and strengthened through identification, or consubstantiality. In this sense the myth becomes synonymous with what public-speaking textbooks call establishing common ground, or rapport. To promote unity among the listeners, the persuader incorporates togetherness devices, "plain folks" appeals, and bandwagon appeals. To drive out discordant members, he may resort to a strategy of terror, scapegoating, and name-calling.

Third, the impact of a myth is influenced by all the factors in the actual speech setting. What appears on the written page often accounts for only a small portion of the persuasive power of the speech as delivered. Very important is the influence of context or atmosphere— the setting, the time, and the staging—as are physical symbols— banners, flags, uniforms, badges, tokens, music, and ritual. These elements are an integral part of the persuasive effort.

Fourth, myths are woven into what traditionally are called ethical and pathetic appeals. Through a myth, a persuader establishes his ethos with the faithful by appearing to be a man of common sense and goodwill. He may further enhance his prestige through participating in the ritual and displaying signs of the legend. He may exhibit a sign of belonging. Southern speakers have made use of Confederate uniforms, lapel pins of flags, and even cotton socks for this purpose. Once achieving the status of a revered leader, the orator who uses a myth sometimes lets his mere presence motivate action. Enjoying a favorable image, the leader, not subject to critical scrutiny, intensifies emotional responses by passing references. To enhance an argument, he uses positively loaded terms. Into a proposition he may plant a single term or phrase to evoke the myth and hence increase the pathetic appeal. Bryan achieved this purpose in the quotation cited above when he said, "The great cities rest upon our *broad and fertile prairies.*" The italicized words bring to mind the agrarian myth.

Fifth, the speaker using a myth builds his persuasion through amplification, utilizing the Aristotelian topic of degree, that is, magnifying and minifying. He is likely to argue in terms of more and less or great and small. He attempts what Aristotle called investing facts and premises with "grandeur and dignity" (Cooper translates the words as "magnitude and beauty").[24] Hence, to accomplish his objective, the persuader builds his arguments and themes around the common virtues and vices; that is, he affirms that his motives, sentiments, and actions are nobler and on a higher plane than those of the opponent. For example, southern speakers emphasized that Confederates fought for freedom, the Constitution, and God, in contrast to the Yankees, who invaded southern homes, sold Negroes for profit, and were un-Christian. They sometimes called up long lists of heroes who personified the great virtues of the group. They amplified their messages by analogy, repetition, maxims, and commonplaces. They knew how to insert "trigger words," slogans, and figurative expressions to activate common myths.

To regard the myth as just another rhetorical device, occasionally inserted into a speech for variety and impressiveness, is to miss its essential nature. Clusters of myths are likely to permeate the whole structure and development of a speech composition and subtly influence and reinforce the total impact. Instead of being an isolated or exclusive device, the myth is a strategy, a mood, or a rhetorical *modus operandi*.

24. J. E. C. Welldon (trans.), *The Rhetoric of Aristotle* (New York, 1886), 70 (Book I, Chap. 9); Lane Cooper (trans.), *The Rhetoric of Aristotle* (New York, 1932), 54.

·····〔 V 〕·····
The Rhetoric of Exploitation
Southern Demagogues in Action

How do the popular leaders commonly designated as demagogues, who held center stage in the South from 1890 to 1970, fit into the region's oral tradition? No less an authority than T. Harry Williams suggests that the South "has produced an inordinate number of them, perhaps more than all other sections of the country together . . . and specifically that South that came into being after the Civil War." [1]

These popular speakers indeed represented a new departure from the antebellum and immediate postbellum leadership in that they took a markedly different approach to the voters and added a rough tone to the prevailing rhetoric. But like their predecessors, they have already become "myth-encrusted," and instead of being remembered as flesh-and-blood speakers, they have been stereotyped and damned for their crudeness and rusticity and misjudged out of context. [2] Often our knowledge of them and their methods comes from opponents such as feature writers for northern publications, historians who favored Bourbon leadership, and conservative editors who delighted in highlighting idiosyncrasies or in denying new leaders fair coverage.

The demagogue sometimes rationalized his methods by saying he was only fighting fire with fire. Admittedly, these speakers were probably no worse as political leaders than some they turned out of office, and their language and tactics were no more extreme. After

1. T. Harry Williams, *Huey Long: A Biography* (New York, 1970), 411.
2. Bernard Mayo, *Myths and Men* (Athens, Ga., 1959), 2–3.

wrestling with this problem, two historians concluded that it "would be better to forget the word [*demagogue*] altogether and to classify politicians . . . as reformers or non-reformers, as progressives or conservatives."[3]

This essay ventilates that loaded term and draws a composite view of the southern demagogic genre and its distinguishing rhetorical strategies. The word *composite* in this context is intended to suggest common tendencies and generalizations about the class instead of exclusive characteristics of specific speakers. Fortunately, the latter task has already been done excellently.[4] This essay discusses seventeen of these popular leaders. These seventeen, mainly from the Deep South, are by no means the only demagogues, and their number could be doubled, particularly if other southern states and minor figures were taken into account. In fact, in what seems an extreme interpretation, some writers have cynically suggested that most twentieth-century southern politicians and orators fit into this category.

The emotionally loaded term *demagogue* comes from the Greek *demagogos* and since ancient times has meant "leader of the people." But almost from the first, *demagogue* took on derogatory connotations. Hence, as a noun it occurs in two contexts: first, as a simple name word for a popular leader who expresses the will of the voters, and second, as a pejorative or disparaging epithet. The entwining of the two senses, a complicating factor in discussing politicians given the label, is of course most evident in popular usage, such as in the press; yet it is also common in dictionaries, reputable histories, and biographies. *The American Political Dictionary* explains that a demagogue is "an unscrupulous politician who seeks to win and hold office through emotional appeals to mass prejudice and passions. Half-truths, outright lies and various means of card stacking may be used in attempts

3. Thomas D. Clark and Albert D. Kirwan, *The South Since Appomattox: A Century of Regional Change* (New York, 1967), 129.
4. Cal M. Logue and Howard Dorgan (eds.), *The Oratory of Southern Demagogues* (Baton Rouge, 1981).

to dupe the voters. Typically, a demagogue may try to win support from one group by blaming another for its misfortunes."[5]

In a scholarly treatise on the subject, Reinhard H. Luthin writes: "He [the demagogue] is a politician skilled in oratory, flattery and invective; evasive in discussing vital issues; promising everything to everybody; appealing to passions rather than the reason of the public; and arousing racial, religious, and class prejudices—a man whose lust for power without recourse to principle leads him to seek to become a master of the masses. He has for centuries practiced his profession of 'man of the people.' He is a product of a political tradition nearly as old as western civilization itself." Among his examples Luthin includes the Populists, William Jennings Bryan, and the Dixie demagogues, devoting full chapters to Theodore G. Bilbo, Eugene Talmadge, and Huey P. Long.[6]

Safire's *Political Dictionary* describes the demagogue as "one who appeals to greed, fear, and hatred; a spellbinding orator, careless with facts and a danger to rational decision." But Safire adds an interesting afterthought. "This [word *demagogue*] is one of the enduring, slashing attack words of politics in use since the American republic began."[7] Realizing this, a stump speaker may attempt with great gusto to render the coup de grace to his opponent by denouncing him as a demagogue.

Such was the practice of the Bourbons, who used this loaded label as a "slashing attack word" to castigate the Populists and progressives, who questioned revered myths, opposed conservative programs, demonstrated popularity with the voters, and thus brought an end to Bourbon rule. Likewise, the demagogues were subjected to the same kind of scorn and harassment.

The above definitions point to a rhetoric of exploitation. In this

5. Jack C. Plano and Milton Greenburg, *The American Political Dictionary* (4th ed.; Hinsdale, Ill., 1976), 118.

6. Reinhard H. Luthin, *American Demagogues: Twentieth Century* (Boston, 1954), 1.

7. William Safire, *Political Dictionary: An Enlarged, Up-to-Date Edition* (New York, 1978), 163.

context, to exploit means to use selfishly for one's own ends, to take advantage of another person's weakness, to gain rewards through manipulation and deception. Examples come readily to mind. The playground bully who grabs candy away from a weaker playmate, the religious leader who under the sanctity of the cloth bleeds his followers for luxurious material possessions, and the clever salesman who applies undue pressure upon an innocent, naïve client to buy what he does not need or cannot afford, are all exploiters.

The rhetoric of exploitation depends upon naïveté and concentrates upon sensitive issues, for example, poverty, prohibition, evolution, religion, immigration, and the race question. Feeding upon emotion, prejudice, and mythic concerns, it attracts listeners and readers who are in the throes of disappointment, frustration, and anxiety, and consequently are searching for easy solutions to their difficulties. Such persons are susceptible to the charismatic leader who outpromises the opposition and offers easy paths to green pastures. Converts are amenable, indeed often eager "to follow and obey," at times responding overtly to the slightest suggestion of a father figure or a "good ole country boy," and even acting violently, going sometimes as far as lynchings.[8]

In every Deep South state, demagogues were preceded in office by an entrenched hierarchy of Bourbon Democrats, or in Huey P. Long's words, "the great white angels of feudal democracy." Having regained power by overturning the Reconstruction regimes, these planters, merchants, bankers, and lawyers monopolized business, industrial, and political activities; made decisions in their closed circles; passed out preferments on their own; and became irate when questioned. T. Harry Williams characterizes the hierarchy and its leaders as "gentlemen in frock coats, string ties, and wide hats . . . [who] gave the state a kind of government like themselves—digni-

8. Eric Hoffer, *The True Believer: Thoughts on the Nature of Mass Movements* (New York, 1951), 109.

fied, usually honest, though sometimes discreetly corrupt, and backward looking."[9]

These gentlemen believed in low taxes, minimum educational and social services, and a laissez-faire policy toward natural resources and industry. They neglected the schools at all levels, permitted convict leasing, saw little wrong with child labor, and did not object to—in fact encouraged—exploitation of poor white and Negro labor. At considerable financial gain to themselves, they disposed of natural resources, mainly timber and iron ore, in transactions with Yankee promoters and permitted the railroad system to fall into the hands of northern capitalists.

After Reconstruction, the Bourbons restored home rule, controlled or disfranchised the black voters, crushed the Republicans, and swallowed up or buried the Populists. They developed the crop lien system and tenant farming. When necessary, they could be corrupt, vindictive, ruthless, and at times as dishonest as those who came before and after them. These Bourbons taught the art of politics to the demagogues, who were willing learners and in many cases later beat the Bourbons at their own games. There is convincing evidence that there would have been no demagogues if the Bourbons had dealt effectively with pressing problems, acted courageously, and provided enlightened leadership in the South.[10]

About 1900, new primary laws forced southern politicians to seek out the voters in the remote hills and piney woods. Under these new conditions, the office seekers had to find different poses, new techniques, and striking new issues to accommodate the rough elements at rural rallies that sometimes became what William Alexander Percy called "obscene pandemonium." Percy described an audience at Lauderdale Springs, Mississippi, that his father faced while campaigning against Vardaman in 1910. When the elder Percy rose to speak, he was greeted with such "a roar of boos, cat calls, hisses and

9. Williams, *Huey Long*, 187.
10. Although many sources verify these conclusions, perhaps the best is C. Vann Woodward, *Origins of the New South, 1877–1913* (Baton Rouge, 1951).

cries of 'Vardaman! Vardaman!'" that "it was impossible to hear a word he might say. The din was insane and intolerable, and it showed no sign of diminishing. Obviously the crowd was determined to make it impossible for him to speak at all." [11]

To appreciate this surly political climate, it helps to remember that politicians were meeting the "pent up redneck rancor" of rural people who were tired of being passed over, starved for representation, envious of the seeming prosperity of their city neighbors, and frustrated by their struggles to grub out sustenance from the overworked, rough acres of their small farms. The politicians had to satisfy the yearnings of these country people for leaders who would talk to them in their own idiom on their own level and who would express violently their boredom, disgust, anxiety, prejudice, and even hate. [12]

Theodore Bilbo, who empathized with his poor white neighbors of south Mississippi, explained their emotions. "Red necks didn't go for" serious speeches, because "life is very dull in the hill country. There are no movies, dances, night clubs, nothing of that sort. And even if there were, people would be too poor to pay for them. So they expect to get their entertainment from preachers and politicians." [13]

In discussing the success of Bilbo and the Longs and men like them, V. O. Key, Jr., observes that "the respectable candidate" was no match against the "rough house tactics of the hell-of-a-fellow, gusty and lusty man"; consequently, "better-element candidates often retired from the fray, beaten, with sombre reflections" that politics was "no game for gentlemen." [14]

These perspectives on what demagogues are said to be and on what conditions spawned them aid in understanding how these mass lead-

11. William Alexander Percy, *Lanterns on the Levee: Recollections of a Planter's Son* (Baton Rouge, 1973), 150–51.

12. Albert D. Kirwan, *Revolt of the Rednecks: Mississippi Politics, 1876–1925* (Lexington, Ky., 1951), 40–49, 93–102, 144–61. See also Clark and Kirwan, *The South Since Appomattox*, 51–81, 108–35.

13. *Newsweek*, August 24, 1935, pp. 19–20.

14. V. O. Key, Jr., *Southern Politics in State and Nation* (New York, 1949), 167.

ers employed a rhetoric of exploitation to achieve their ends. In every case from Tillman to Wallace, these southern mavericks followed a strategy of aligning the have-nots, namely the poor rural masses, against the entrenched hierarchy and elite.

They became masters at establishing the impression that they were "just one of the boys," or at making "plain folks" appeals. In other words, they knew that identification constitutes powerful persuasion. In putting their acts on the road, they became master showmen, striking characters, and tireless campaigners. They demonstrated a "bold, dashing, hell-of-a-fellow complex," or they posed as "good ole boys." They made sure that their listeners would not forget them, especially on election day.[15]

To promote identification, they exuded signs of rusticity through their dress, countrified language and manners, and amusing antics. They frequently inserted into their speeches testimony of their personal knowledge of the joys, hardships, and sorrows of rural living. They expressed delight in rural folkways, country music, hoedowns, farm cooking, doing the chores, and good old-time religion. They gave credence to the folk wisdom that "it is possible to take the boy out of the country, but not the country out of the boy."

Brief sketches of seven of these politicians will suggest how they attracted constituencies. All seventeen popular leaders mentioned herein were remarkably alike in many of their antics and programs. This is not surprising, since they often looked to one another for support, and adapted techniques from one another for use in their own states.

In South Carolina in the 1880s, after years of antagonism between the upland farmers and a hierarchy composed of the planters and the Charleston elite, "a real dirt farmer" by the name of Ben Tillman (1847–1918) came thundering out of rough Edgefield County. He possessed none of the polish or eloquence of a Bourbon aristocrat,

15. W. J. Cash, *The Mind of the South* (New York, 1941), 246–56.

showed little respect for the cult of the Lost Cause, and had no desire to join the upper class. He billed himself as "an old plowboy," "a clod-hopper," and "nothing but a barnyard rooster." He made his stand perfectly clear, bragging, "I'm one of you boys and own to it," and denouncing "the pot gutted blue bloods" and "the broken down aristocrats" who suck the "public teat." No one had ever dared to be so harsh or disrespectful toward General Wade Hampton and the "southern gentlemen" and in urging "the masses of the people" to revolt against "the oligarchy of office seekers, a codfish aristocracy based on money and brass."

Not a handsome man, Tillman had a coarse face and an empty eye socket, and he once told the United States Senate, "I am a rude man and don't care." He made angry and frank speeches about agricultural woes and the aristocrats. A sign of his honesty can be found in his admission that "I do not deny that I played politics and through sheer necessity I acted the demagogue at times; because I was opposed so unscrupulously I had to defend myself and fight the devil with fire."

During his first campaign for the governorship of South Carolina, Tillman debated his opponents in every county in the state and seldom passed up other opportunities to speak to farmers' meetings. The Agricultural Moses addressed thirty-two to thirty-five meetings during the three summer months in each of his three campaigns for governor (1890, 1892, and 1894). In 1892, Tillman spoke face-to-face to at least fifty-five thousand persons. After he went to the Senate, he frequently returned to the Palmetto State for politicking and also traveled outside the state to deliver many political and chautauqua addresses. In fact, in his last active tour of the state in 1906, he made twenty-one speeches to more than fifty-two thousand people in less than a month.[16]

Eugene Talmadge of Georgia, or "Ol' Gene" (1884–1946), was a wiry, weather-beaten, lean, dark-skinned dirt farmer and lawyer who had an owlish look because of his enormous round-framed glasses. He

16. Lindsey Saunders Perkins, "The Oratory of Benjamin Ryan Tillman" (Ph.D. dissertation, Northwestern University, 1945), 39, 46, 67, 101, 437–64.

sought dramatic moments to show off his red suspenders that matched his red bandanna, which he often held in hand. To establish himself as "a real dirt farmer," Ol' Gene sometimes called to the platform several friends to testify that they had actually seen him in the field plowing with a mule. In the best country style, he could spit tobacco with accuracy and drink corn liquor from a jug. Upon becoming governor in 1933, he had a chicken pen built in back of the mansion and pastured an old milk cow on the lawn. His wife Mitt played her supporting role well by digging up wild onions from the front yard of the mansion. She let the reporters know that she much preferred her farm home to the governor's mansion. Ol' Gene invited his rural listeners to Atlanta, saying, "Come see me and Mitt at the mansion and we'll spit tobacco over the porch railing." He used earthier versions when he was just among the boys. "Come see me at the mansion. We'll sit on the front porch and we'll spit tobacco and we'll ——— over the rail on those city bastards." His biographer appraises Ol' Gene, known in Georgia as the Wild Man from Sugar Creek, as "fiery, indignant, angry, corny, and iconoclastic." Probably no other southern politician was more rustic, uncouth, or profane than this man who was elected governor of Georgia three times.[17]

In Arkansas, quaint Jeff Davis (1862–1913), billing himself as a hillbilly lawyer, battled "the silk stocking or the high collared crowd," by which he meant the lawyers, editors, and businessmen in Little Rock. At one rally, for example, he told the farmers that he "had rather eat turnip greens, hog jowls and cornbread with you fellows out here than go into the hotel and eat with the high collared crowd." Building a "one-gallus" image, Davis was an enormous man, a "carrot haired, red faced, loud mouthed, strong limbed, ox driving, mountaineer lawyer." He wore a Confederate gray Prince Albert suit, a Baptist black tie, wool socks, a broad-brimmed gray Stetson, and

17. William Anderson, *The Wild Man from Sugar Creek: The Political Career of Eugene Talmadge* (Baton Rouge, 1975), 42, 82, 98, 103–104; Sarah McCulloh Lemmon, "The Public Career of Eugene Talmadge, 1926–1936" (Ph.D. dissertation, University of North Carolina, 1952).

red suspenders. While speaking, he was likely to lay aside his coat at a moment that demanded emphasis. Often at the urging of a listener, he showed off his red galluses or called attention to his socks, bragging that they were "the kind you farmers wear."

When he wanted to be eloquent about rustic charm, he could draw from a repertory of choice bits. For example, on one occasion he said:

> I dressed and went on the front porch, looking down the hillside and valleys; there I saw Nature robed with all its beauty. I . . . saw the cattle on the hillside; I looked . . . and saw more than a dozen bee-gums. I looked into the cow lot, and there I saw more than a half dozen loads of manure piled up and on the right was more than three cords of stove wood placed in proper order. The house was beautifully painted, "the old oaken bucket, the iron bound bucket, the moss covered bucket which hangs in the well," was in the proper place. The chickens were flying down from the hen roosts; the sun was rising in the eastern horizon and kissing the morning dew drops. Ah, ladies and gentlemen, there was a beautiful picture of Nature in all its glory.

From the time that he sought the post of attorney general of Arkansas in 1898, through three successful canvasses for governor between 1900 and 1904 and two for the United States Senate in 1906 and 1912, Jeff Davis campaigned all over the state, including in its remotest villages, often traveling under difficult conditions over rough terrain. In 1900, in his first try for governor, he spoke 120 times, including 38 debates with opponents. In 1902, he spoke 140 times, including 70 debates with his Republican challenger. In his third try for the governorship, he spoke 160 times. To counter an unfriendly press, he distributed his speeches widely in pamphlet form, passing out 125,000 copies in 1900.[18]

In Mississippi, Vardaman, Bilbo, and Barnett warred upon the

18. Billy Travis Booth, "An Analysis of the Myths in Selected Speeches of Jeff Davis of Arkansas, 1899–1911" (M.A. thesis, Louisiana State University, 1977); L. S. Dunaway, *Jeff Davis, Governor and U.S. Senator: His Life and Speeches* (Little Rock, 1913), 32; John Richard Johnson, "The Campaign Speaking of Jeff Davis of Arkansas, 1899–1904" (M.A. thesis, Louisiana State University, 1974).

delta planters and the Jackson and Gulf Coast elite, seeking the support of the hill farmers in the northeastern part of the state and the farmers of the piney woods to the south. Bilbo expressed the conflict succinctly when he opened his campaign for lieutenant governor in 1910. "Don't mistake the issue," he said. "The fight between the classes and the masses, between corporate influence and the people, is on and it will be a fight to the finish." [19]

James K. Vardaman (1861–1930), "the White Chief" of Mississippi, was unique among the demagogues, not because of what he advocated, but for his natty appearance and manner. Dressing like a dandy, Vardaman had a "majestic stature, a massive head and deep brown eyes" and was fastidious and vain about his grooming, wearing his black hair (which, it is reported, he brushed a hundred times a day) shoulder length. With the exception of a wide-brimmed Stetson, he dressed all in white, including his shoes. Sometimes he sported a carnation in his lapel. Strange as it may seem, "while posing as a commoner, he acted the part of an aristocrat, and Mississippians liked it." In spite of his dress he did not mind riding to a rally in a wagon pulled by oxen. [20]

In 1903, Vardaman, appearing at "barbecues, church festivals, camp meetings, county fairs and political pow wows," was reported to have delivered seven hundred speeches over a fourteen-month period. During these expeditions he shook hands with "legions of men, bowed gracefully to noble women," and "kissed car-loads of babies." [21] For the next twenty years he continued this regimen.

Theodore "The Man" Bilbo (1877–1947), a decided contrast to his mentor Vardaman, was a diminutive man, five feet two inches tall, but he was regarded as a giant at rallies. Looking the part of a country boy, the little fellow with a broad head traveled about rural

19. *Mississippi Free Press* (Poplarville, Miss.), April 21, 1910. See also Key, *Southern Politics*, 230–33.

20. William F. Holmes, *The White Chief: James Kimble Vardaman* (Baton Rouge, 1970), 108; Kirwan, *Revolt of the Rednecks*, 145.

21. Jackson *Clarion Ledger*, September 15, 1903.

Mississippi wearing loud check suits or dirty out-of-style cottons and sporting two trademarks: a red necktie and a horseshoe-shaped stickpin set with thirty-nine diamonds. Exuding considerable pride in The Man, his local admirers described him as "a slick little bastard." One reporter wrote that "as a phenomenon in politics Bilbo was as American as chewin' tobacco." Probably even more active than the White Chief, Bilbo might speak a thousand times during a canvass, appearing five to eight times a day and on some occasions holding forth for two hours or more. He had a goal of speaking in every county and being seen "in nearly every hamlet in the state." [22]

Louisiana has had more than its share of quaint and spectacular stumpers, including Huey and Earl Long, Jimmie Davis, John McKeithen, Leander Perez, "Coozan" Dudley LeBlanc, and on and on. In this company, Huey P. Long, "The Kingfish" (1893–1935), was by far the most dramatic and successful. According to T. Harry Williams, "His features were a cartoonist's delight—exaggerated, comic and yet impressive." Arthur Schlesinger, Jr., described his face as "round, red, and blotched, with more than a hint of pouches and jowls. . . . At times, it was the face of the cunning yokel. . . . At times, it became exceedingly hard and cruel." [23]

Huey put on a good show for his rural admirers. He could clown, tell a good story, rib an opponent, and most important, make his bold talk relevant to his listeners, often calling onlookers by name and expressing concern about their plights. Williams demonstrates how Huey set off the poor from the rich. In speech after speech, in every parish, Long would declare, "I don't want the bosses. I want the people on my side. There's going to be a new day in Louisiana." He

22. *Newsweek*, September 1, 1947, p. 19, August 25, 1935, p. 10. See also Dorothy Jefferson Merrill, "The Speaking of Theodore G. Bilbo in the 1934 Mississippi Senatorial Campaign" (M.A. thesis, Louisiana State University, 1950); A. W. Green, *The Man Bilbo* (Baton Rouge, 1963); Larry Thomas Bulsamo, "Theodore G. Bilbo and Mississippi Politics, 1877–1932" (Ph.D. dissertation, University of Missouri, 1967).

23. Williams, *Huey Long*, 200; Henry C. Dethloff (ed.), *Huey P. Long: Southern Demagogue or American Democrat?* (Boston, 1967), 80.

might say: "Now, Mr. Gilbert [the parish boss], I don't want your vote. There is no reason why you should vote for me. You are a rich man. You own all the land around here. You have all these poor devils working for you. . . . I am trying to help these poor fellows that you are giving a raw deal. I want the vote of these peapickers that have come to hear me talk."[24] According to Hodding Carter, Huey, a "most indefatigable campaigner," was "the best-catch-as-catch-can-stumper" in the South. In 1924, over mud and gravel roads and across many ferries, he traveled 15,000 miles by automobile, speaking three to five times a day and reaching probably 300,000 listeners.[25] He also introduced the technique of the mass-media blitz into his campaign. In 1930, to improve his coverage, he bought two sound trucks that leapfrogged along his campaign route. While he spoke from one, the other went on ahead to the next stop to announce his arrival and attract listeners with recorded country music.

Huey also made use of direct mailing, handbills, circulars (distributing over twenty-six million in the course of his career), posters, and later his own newspaper, the *Progress*. In the midst of a canvass, he might have thousands of handbills printed in Baton Rouge and carried throughout the state by the state police. He once bragged, "A document prepared by me in the evening could be printed and placed on the porch of practically every home in the state of Louisiana during the morning of the following day." He frequently reached his supporters over radio, especially from KWKH in Shreveport, and later over national networks, when as a United States senator he was promoting his Share Our Wealth program. No other politician of his time made such effective use of the media as the Kingfish.[26]

His little brother Earl (1895–1960), known in Louisiana as Uncle

---

24. Williams, *Huey Long*, 181–82.
25. Hodding Carter, "Huey Long: American Dictator," in *The Aspirin Age, 1919–1941*, ed. Isabel Leighton (New York, 1949), 348–49.
26. Key, *Southern Politics*, 162; Ernest G. Bormann, "A Rhetorical Analysis of the National Radio Broadcasts of Senator Huey P. Long" (Ph.D. dissertation, University of Iowa, 1953).

Earl and, according to his own words, the Last of the Red Hot Papas, was likewise no slouch at attracting crowds. In contrasting himself with Huey, Earl suggested that he was "more or less opposite. . . . I'm the slow plodding type and Huey was quick, and ready for action at all times." No one fit the stereotype of a "good ole country boy" better than this disheveled old man, with his folksy speech and his gravel voice. He often appeared on the stump coatless, wearing an old pair of baggy tan pants held up by galluses, sometimes with only one fastened, and a badly wrinkled, sweaty white shirt, open at the collar and bagging halfway out of his pants. He liked cowboy boots, of which he supposedly had around three hundred pairs. Hanging carelessly out of a back pocket or waving in his hand was his favorite colored bandanna, with which he casually mopped his sweaty face while talking. Sometimes when listening to other speakers, he would soak his handkerchief with Coke and spread it over his face. In his last campaign in 1960, just before his death, he assured his listeners in a typical Earl Long comment, "They say I'm worn out but I've got some snap left and some in my garters, too."[27]

Earl was as active a campaigner as Huey. While Huey was alive, Earl played mainly a subsidiary role, doing practical politicking and what he called "keeping him [Huey] out of trouble." But in 1932 Earl launched out on his own, campaigning for lieutenant governor. He crisscrossed the state several times on each of his tries for office. With his homespun manner, Earl knew how to amble along, pause at a roadside stand, visit at country stores, and chat with passersby. He carefully kept in touch with his many buddies in each parish of the state. His opponent Sam Jones once observed that Earl's secret was that he "had lots of friends . . . little friends. . . . Earl would keep strength among people that the average politician didn't pay attention to. These people just wanted recognition and didn't want anything else. Earl knew people . . . and their weaknesses."[28]

27. Baton Rouge *Morning Advocate*, January 19, 1956; Alexandria (La.) *Town Talk*, July 4, 1960.
28. New Orleans *Times Picayune*, June 22, 1939; Richard McCaughan, *Socks on a Rooster: Louisiana's Earl K. Long* (Baton Rouge, 1967), 155.

In addition to the seven demagogues just described, there were others who were equally colorful, rustic, and corny. It is difficult to forget Tom Watson, whose ranting on the platform and in his magazines fascinated Georgians for over thirty years; Cole Blease of South Carolina, who as governor openly advocated lynching; the bigot Tom Heflin of Alabama, who was an oratorical exhibitionist of the first order; profane Cotton Ed Smith of South Carolina, who rode to rallies atop a wagonload of cotton bales to the tune of "Dixie"; the six-foot-eight giant, Jim Folsom, who clapped and stomped while his country band, the Strawberry Pickers, was beating out his own tunes, "Way Down Yonder" or "Y'all Come"; and Louisiana's singing governor, Jimmie Davis, who rode his horse up the capitol steps and sang his own "You Are My Sunshine" to the state legislators.

In comparison with their infamous predecessors the popular southern governors of the 1960s did not fall short in dramatics: Alabama's pugilistic George Wallace, standing symbolically at the door of a building at the University of Alabama to block the admission of a lonely black applicant; Mississippi's Ross Barnett, the tool of the White Citizens' Councils, fanning the flames of hatred and mob violence throughout his state and at the University of Mississippi; Arkansas' Orval Faubus, selfishly complicating for political gain the integration of Central High School in Little Rock by permitting and promoting harassment of nine lonely black students and their troubled teachers; and Georgia's clownish Lester Maddox, riding his bicycle backward or waving his ax handle in front of his Pickrick Restaurant in Atlanta while spouting his political and religious primitivism.

The southern demagogues, contrary to the impression that they worked so hard to convey by their crude language, uncouth manners, and funny clothes, were not ignorant or stupid country rubes. They may have been prejudiced and sometimes unethical, but they were far from being simple-minded and ill-informed. Shrewd, calculating strategists, they knew what they wanted and steered fixed courses toward their goals.

Thirteen of the seventeen discussed here had attended college; twelve were admitted to the bar, though Heflin and Vardaman did not practice extensively; three were principally editors (Watson, Faubus, and Vardaman). Only two came from homes in the lower middle class (Maddox and Jimmie Davis). But none could claim being poor whites, and none had been subjected to the deprivations that many of their supporters had experienced. Indeed, Tillman, Watson, Talmadge, and Cotton Ed Smith owned substantial farmland. Folsom had been a successful insurance salesman; Maddox was the owner of a restaurant that at one time grossed $500,000 per year; and Jimmie Davis, who had a master's degree, was a millionaire country musician and composer.

In posing as "good ole boys," these speakers often took on the characteristics of actors, medicine men, and con artists. Their behavior suggested that their models were sideshow barkers, country preachers, and revival-tent-style evangelists. They made no attempt to achieve the polish of the Old South's famous deliberative orators or the New South's ceremonial speakers. Instead, they were likely to copy one another and imitate demagogues from other sections, adapting whatever enhanced their own techniques of persuasion. Not concerned with explaining or clarifying issues or with rational decision making, they sought to convey images and to arouse immediate, violent emotions and overt passions. They did not mind being thought of as clowns, for they wanted to entertain the red-necks, arouse the disgust of their upper-class critics, and draw the scorn of the conservative press.

Nevertheless, when the occasion demanded, most of these "good ole boys" could shed their sloppy clothes and appear in neat, conservative business suits, speaking cogently and grammatically to sophisticated groups. In Washington they often forgot their rustic poses and conformed to the gentlemanly behavior of the Senate, except when the galleries were filled with expectant onlookers.

These popular leaders devised strategies and programs that constituted a rhetoric of exploitation. "Glib and shameless," and always sensitive to rural yearnings and problems, these "men of the people," through "wit and cunning," outpromised, outmuscled, and outmaneuvered the conservatives. They outdistanced their opponents by proposing radical reforms always denounced by the ruling oligarchs but indeed alluring to the voters. And with the exception of Bilbo and the Longs, the so-called demagogues usually promised far more than they could deliver.[29]

They advocated improved education and more social services for whites, larger old-age pensions, stricter regulation of corporations and railroads, reform of state government, elimination of monopolies, improvement of prisons, an end to convict leasing, more lenient pardoning, better roads (and more bridges in Louisiana), free textbooks for students, cheap automobile licenses, more equitable distribution of tax burdens, reduced utility rates, better health care, improvements in agricultural practices, and more efficient administrations. The ultimate among their proposals was Huey P. Long's Share Our Wealth scheme, which promised to make "every man a king." Advanced during the Great Depression, this program attracted a national following for the Kingfish.

With the exception of the Longs and Folsom, these politicians decried attempts to improve the lot of the Negroes, particularly in the areas of social welfare and higher education. They urged that the blacks be kept on the plantations as field hands and housemaids.

The demagogues were the heirs apparent of the Populists in their platforms as well as their followings. Like their predecessors, these neo-Populists made scapegoats of Wall Street, big business, the railroads, monopolies, the wealthy, and officeholders. One of Huey P. Long's favorite targets was Standard Oil of New Jersey. Jeff Davis attacked the fire insurance companies. Tom Heflin denounced the cotton trust and Wall Street. Ben Tillman attacked the state agricultural bureau, the University of South Carolina, and the Citadel. George Wallace lashed out at the "multi-billion dollar foundations" and the "multi-millionaire property holders." James Folsom ran against "the Big Mules"—the industrial leaders of Birmingham and Mobile—and dramatized his disgust with the Establishment by mak-

29. Clark and Kirwan, *The South Since Appomattox*, 108–35; Percy, *Lanterns on the Levee*, 140–54.

ing a mop and suds bucket the symbol of his campaign, saying, "You give me suds [donations], I'll do the scouring at the capital."

In spite of their Populist leanings, all of these popular leaders except Thomas Watson remained within the Democratic party throughout their careers. They simply pushed aside the Bourbons with the assistance of loyal rural support. Huey Long actually built his own political machine from the parish level upward.

On the basis of their followings, many moved up the political ladder to Washington to serve terms in the United States Senate. Vardaman became a progressive but opposed the entrance of the United States into World War I. Bilbo became an ardent New Dealer and backer of Franklin D. Roosevelt. Long first supported the New Deal and FDR, but later, in opposition to Roosevelt's programs, he proposed his Share Our Wealth plan.

Some turned reactionary. Tillman became rigidly conservative in his last years in the Senate. Talmadge became a bitter foe of the New Deal, resented the interference of the federal government in Georgia's affairs, and considered running against FDR in a third party. Watson, always highly influential in Georgia politics, became a kind of power broker, shifting from faction to faction as whim struck him. As an old man, he entered the Senate on the Democratic ticket in order to oppose the League of Nations and the World Court.

Perhaps the editorial in the Atlanta *Constitution* at the death of Eugene Talmadge could be applied to most of the seventeen. After describing Ol' Gene as "a puzzling and frequently contradictory . . . legendary and almost fabulous character," the writer, in what appeared to be almost a lament, said that "the Georgia scene would seem strange and empty without him." So it was when the others departed.[30]

The foremost rhetorical strategy of southern demagogues was their wanton exploitation of deep-seated racism. In contrast to the milder, paternalistic Bourbons, they specialized in ridicule, name-calling, character assassination, and lurid descriptions of rape and violence.

30. Atlanta *Constitution*, December 22, 1946.

They made scapegoats of Negroes, Catholics, and Jews. Touching raw emotion and festering anxieties, they sometimes turned their audiences into mobs who expressed their passion in harassment, burning, and, in the extreme, lynching. Of course, they became fellow travelers with the Klan, the White Citizens' Councils, and other racist zealots. They usually denied that they condoned mobocracy. But once a mob took over, they could do little to quell it, although some occasionally tried—Vardaman, for example.

V. O. Key observes, "It is a puzzling characteristic of southern politics that candidates can at times get themselves elected by their skill in advocating something on which every one is agreed." Thus, "nigger baiting" elected many southern politicians from the end of Reconstruction until at least 1970. Cotton Ed Smith is reported to have pushed white supremacy the hardest in years when cotton prices were low, in order to direct the farmers' attention away from their economic woes.[31]

The mass leaders based their Negrophobia on four common themes: the Negro is inferior, he must be "kept in his place," equal education is a waste of money, and the only effective control over the Negro's natural criminality is lynching. The only means to preserve "the southern way of life," therefore, was through the maintenance of separation of the races. None of these arguments were new, but the southern leaders always found willing ears among the rural whites, closest to the blacks on the economic ladder.

Vardaman, Blease, and Cotton Ed Smith were the most extreme of the lot. After unsuccessful attempts to break into Bourbon political machines, Vardaman turned to racism; and for twenty years in his editorials in the Greenwood *Commonwealth* and his other newspapers and in his speeches on the stump, he fanned racial hatred. He preached that the "negro is the same as he was five thousand years ago" and that the black's proper occupations were as field hands and housemaids on plantations away from the cities. He was determined that "the negro . . . will not be permitted to rise above the station which

31. Key, *Southern Politics*, 232; Allan A. Michie and Frank Ryhlick, *Dixie Demagogues* (New York, 1939), 267.

he now fills."[32] The White Chief found a most responsive chord when he openly condoned lynching as a means of controlling lawlessness. Playing upon the reverence for southern ladies that was so much a part of the southern mystique, Vardaman preached that red-blooded men had no choice but to protect the fair ones from the depraved brutes. His glorification of southern women went hand in hand with his lurid descriptions of Negro crimes and the resulting lynchings.[33] At Crystal Springs in 1903, he made his position clear: "I want to tell you just how far I am in favor of mob law. If I were the sheriff and a negro [rapist] fell into my hands, I would run him out of the county. If I were governor and were asked for troops to protect him, I would send them. But if I were a private citizen, I would lead the mob to string the brute up."[34]

Blease, who followed Tillman in South Carolina and built his support mainly among mill workers and farmers, exceeded even Vardaman in his exploitation of Negrophobia. In his first inaugural address, which had the "tone of a stump speech," Blease stated: "This is a white man's country and will continue to be ruled by the white man, regardless of the opinions or editorials of a [sic] quarter or half breeds or foreigners. The pure blooded Caucasian will always defend the virtues of our women. No matter what the cost, if rape is committed, death must follow." In December, 1912, he told a governor's conference, "Whenever the Constitution of my state steps between me and the defense of the virtue of the white women of my state . . . then I say to hell with the Constitution."[35]

Some southern speakers waited until well into their careers to turn

32. Eugene E. White, "The Speaking of James K. Vardaman in the Mississippi Gubernatorial Campaign of 1903" (M.A. thesis, Louisiana State University, 1944), 27–28, 67–68.

33. For Vardaman's account of a lynching in Corinth, Mississippi, see Greenwood *Commonwealth*, October 10, 1902, quoted in Holmes, *The White Chief*, 89.

34. Okolona (Miss.) *Sun*, July 30, 1903, quoted in White, "The Speaking of Vardaman," 14.

35. Ronald Danton Burnside, "The Governorship of Coleman Livingston Blease of South Carolina, 1911–1915" (Ph.D. dissertation, Indiana University, 1963), 40; *Literary Digest*, XLV (1912), 1164–65; *Independent*, LXXIII (1912), 1383–84.

to ardent appeals to Negrophobia. When they found other strategies less effective or experienced a decline in their popularity, they would turn to rampant "nigger baiting." This observation certainly holds true in the cases of Watson, Tillman, Bilbo, and contemporary figures Wallace, Maddox, Faubus, and Barnett.

Watson serves as a good example of the tendency. Prior to 1896, as a Populist, he attempted to unite Negro and white farmers in common cause and spoke to mixed gatherings repeatedly from the same platform with Negro speakers. However, he met with failure and vicious attacks for his racial moderation. After his defeat for the vice-presidency in 1896 on the Populist ticket, he withdrew from political activities for eight years. Upon his return in 1904, Watson cynically concluded that the only answer to his political problems was to eliminate the purchasable Negro vote by disfranchisement. From that time on, he gave Negrophobia as well as hatred of Catholics and Jews central focus in his speaking and editorial activities.

Upon entering South Carolina politics in the middle eighties, Tillman concentrated his speaking on agricultural reform and upon lambasting the entrenched officeholders. In his battles with the conservatives, Tillman saw the black vote used against him; consequently, as governor he led the move to rewrite the state constitution in order to disfranchise the black voter. When he entered the United States Senate in 1894, he kept the home fires burning by his often shocking racial pronouncements and imposed his remarks about the race issue "upon the usually unwilling ears of Senators" forced to listen to his tirades on the Senate floor. In addition, he gave many lyceum and chautauqua lectures to curious northern audiences who wanted to see the violent man from South Carolina.

Bilbo entered Mississippi politics as a supporter of Vardaman; consequently, the voters knew that he was solid in his racial attitudes. Therefore The Man did not seem to exploit racial rhetoric during his first years of stumping. By the twenties, when he sensed that he was losing popularity, he began to make use of Negrophobia. Once in the United States Senate, he became watchdog to "the Mississippi way of life," making pronouncements for home consumption on antilynching legislation, the movement to do away with the poll tax, and the activities of the Fair Employment Practices Commission. He explained that he did not hate Negroes "who stayed in the negro's place," but he became violent about racial mixing. On May 4, 1946, during his last campaign, he told an audience at Pontotoc: "Personally I had rather see my race destroyed with the noted atomic bomb than to see it gradually destroyed within 300 years by mongrelization of the white and black races. The only difference is the atomic bomb would do it instantly and mongrelization is done slowly [but] just as surely." In 1944, he warned the Mississippi legislature, "Practicing social equality of the races is certainly the surest way to destroy the culture of the white race." He also saw "a systematic warfare being waged in many quarters against southern tradition and customs."[36]

Wallace, Maddox, and Barnett were more or less moderate in their early careers, but they later achieved greater success through their rhetoric on segregation. Wallace started out on the moderate side, working for Big Jim Folsom, who was a moderate. When he lost the governorship to John Patterson in 1958, Wallace changed, saying: "John Patterson out-nigguhed me. And boys, I am not going to be out-nigguhed again."[37] And he was true to his word. In his inaugural address of 1962, which has been termed "one of the most belligerent ever given in the modern South," the little man announced: "Segregation now, segregation tomorrow, segregation forever." He used racial rhetoric in every campaign thereafter. Maddox was an unsuccessful politician until he stood in the door of his Pickrick Restaurant, threatening blacks with an ax handle. That gesture made him famous, and racial rhetoric also became his trademark.

The three major rhetorical strategies employed by the southern demagogues, then, were their persistent "plain folks" appeals, their neo-

36. Quoted in Thurston Ermon Doler, "Theodore G. Bilbo's Rhetoric on Race Relations" (Ph.D. dissertation, University of Oregon, 1968), 194; Theodore G. Bilbo, Speech before the Mississippi Legislature, in *Congressional Record*, 78th Cong., 2nd Sess., appendix, A1800.

37. Marshall Frady, *Wallace* (New York, 1976), 127.

Populist programs, and their race-baiting. But to suggest that they were the sole users of a rhetoric of exploitation is to overlook a common practice of many other overzealous politicians, dating from as far back as ancient Greece. Often it has happened that hard-pressed popular leaders have resorted to rabble-rousing in order to get quick, favorable responses. Such was the case with the southern leaders discussed herein. Conditions in the South from 1890 to 1970 provided a relatively large number of the type for case studies of this rhetorical genre.

With some justification these men of the people rationalized that they were only "fighting fire with fire" and that extreme means were necessary to cope with the political machines that they faced. But regardless of the ends intended and achieved, the rhetoric of exploitation is based upon a cynical view of the capacities of the voters and of democratic society and its cherished ideals. It destroys human dignity and human rights, and places passions above rationality. It is based upon the assumptions that constituents must be reached through the simplest and basest appeals, that they cannot be trusted to choose the better of alternatives, that they are incapable of deciding what is good for them, and that the politician has intuitive insights not available to the average man.

Furthermore, such rhetoric easily becomes flawed when the elected official puts personal ambitions or desires above the welfare of the governed. Once power is tasted, the exploiter may forget his promises and turn his energies toward finding ways to stay in office and to enjoy the continuing adoration of his faithful followers. Under these conditions the boldest reformer easily becomes a mediocre executive or an ineffective legislator.

Many of the so-called southern demagogues had laudable goals and did achieve some progressive reforms—mainly beneficial to the white population. Admittedly, in some cases they had better records than their predecessors. On the negative side, after receiving substantial mandates from the lower classes, they did not come up to their potential in instituting meaningful social and economic change. In the end, they were better showmen than they were reformers.

Accompanying their rhetoric of exploitation were crudity, violence, and mobocracy. They not only drove out conservative leadership, but they also stifled creative reformers. They stirred up deep opposition and helped breed cynicism and distrust toward the political process, leaving residues of ill will and even hatred between races and classes. They fomented difficult problems for others to solve, and under their leadership their states failed to match the progress made by states in other sections.

···❦⟨ VI ⟩❧···

The Rhetoric
of a Closed Society

On November 7, 1963, in a presidential address before the Southern Historical Association meeting in Asheville, North Carolina, James W. Silver, then professor of history at the University of Mississippi, labeled his state "a closed society." Reflecting upon the prevailing turmoil there, he said: "In such a society a never ceasing propagation of the 'true faith' must and has gone on relentlessly with a constantly reiterated demand for loyalty to the united front demanding that nonconformists be hushed, silenced with a vengeance, or in crisis situations driven from the community. Violence and the threat of violence have reinforced the presumption of unanimity."[1] The purpose of this essay is to provide some insights into the rhetoric of the closed society described by Silver.

At the outset it is necessary to clarify two principal terms. In this context *rhetoric* is not confined to its traditional scope of verbal and rational communication as defined in Aristotle's *Rhetoric*. The term must include extrinsic appeals that Aristotle placed outside the speaker's art. The total rhetorical campaign encompasses manipulation of the setting, control of the media, and exploitation of emotion. This kind of rhetoric includes coercion and even terror. Involved are group strategies in addition to those directed toward the individual.

1. James W. Silver, "Mississippi: The Closed Society," *Journal of Southern History*, XXX (1964), 3–34. Silver expanded this address into a book by the same title. See the following footnote.

The second term, *closed society*, may apply to a region, a state, an ethnic group, a neighborhood, a cult, a team, a religious order, a gang, a church congregation, a lodge, a fraternity, or even a family. When people develop strong ethnic, philosophical, and emotional ties and act together without questioning, they approach oneness, or what Kenneth Burke has called consubstantiality. They accept common articles of faith and respond to common symbols and ritual. They control the means of communication and limit access to outside information. They regiment and discipline the membership, silencing and ostracizing opposition. They act in response to the slightest suggestion from an opinion leader. Once an action is launched, the members move forward together, reinforcing one another and intensifying emotional involvement.[2]

The state of Mississippi during the decade from 1954 to 1964 was an excellent example of a closed society. Perhaps more than any of its neighbors, this state after 1865 resisted the mainstream of American development and continuously strengthened its introversion. Poverty, ignorance, and the heavy concentrations of blacks in key counties provided white opinion leaders with means to promote cohesiveness among the white population. Retreating into a mythical past, Mississippians held dear the legends of the Old South, the Lost Cause, and the Solid South. The state officially observed Confederate Memorial Day and the birthdays of Robert E. Lee and Jefferson Davis. Walter Lord describes the attachment to the past. "Schoolboys loved to dress up in uniforms . . . older men wistfully told how it all might have been different if only Pemberton had held at Champion Hill. . . . Confederate flags hung from porches all over the state; and in case anyone ever needed reminding, there was always the reproachful

2. James W. Silver, *Mississippi: The Closed Society* (New enlarged ed.; New York, 1966), 6. These characteristics were abstracted from Silver and were based upon a synthesis of reading about the Nazis and Fascists. Many of these same characteristics were evident in the tragic events surrounding the People's Temple of Jim Jones. Asked about the origin of the phrase "the closed society," Silver replied, "I haven't the faintest idea how 'the closed society' got into my head." He thinks that he first used the phrase in the 1950s. Letter to author, October 5, 1979.

gaze of the noble stone soldier who stood atop the Confederate monument in every courthouse square."[3]

The most sacrosanct ideals of white Mississippians were white supremacy and racial segregation. "No candidate, no campaign, no election, no administration has escaped the issue; most of them were dominated by it. . . . In one way or another the biracial nature of the population . . . provided the dynamics for political action in Mississippi since 1850."[4]

During the administration of Ross R. Barnett (1960–1964), with the influence of the White Citizens' Council at its peak, the state reached the ultimate in closedness. Neil R. McMillen points out, "Indeed, by forging political alliances and adroitly manipulating public opinion, it [the White Citizens' Council] managed so thoroughly to obscure all distinctions between public and private authority that by the early sixties the organization was the almost unchallenged arbiter of Mississippi politics." The ruckus over the entry of James Meredith to the University of Mississippi demonstrated the extremes to which the zealots were willing to go to keep their control.[5]

Admittedly, Mississippi never approached the degree of closedness that existed in Nazi Germany, the People's Temple of Jim Jones, and many secret societies. Never was there a time when official orthodoxy was not challenged by a few brave editors such as Hodding Carter of the Greenville *Delta Democrat-Times*, Oliver Emmerich of the McComb *Enterprise-Journal*, and Hazel Brannon Smith of the Jackson

---

3. Walter Lord, *The Past That Would Not Die* (London, 1966), 35.

4. Charles N. Fortenberry and F. Glenn Abney, "Mississippi: Unreconstructed and Unredeemed," in *The Changing Politics of the South*, ed. William C. Havard (Baton Rouge, 1972), 472–524. For further discussions on the political climate in Mississippi during the period, see Lord, *The Past That Would Not Die*, 1–59; Jack Bass and Walter DeVries, *The Transformation of Southern Politics* (New York, 1976), 186–217; Neil R. McMillen, "Development of Civil Rights, 1956–1970," in *A History of Mississippi*, ed. Richard A. McLemore (2 vols.; Hattiesburg, 1973), II, 155–65.

5. McMillen, "Development of Civil Rights," 159; Silver, *Mississippi*, 107–33.

Northside Reporter and Lexington *Advocate*; outspoken professors such as Silver; writers such as William Faulkner and Florence Mars; courageous ministers like Duncan N. Gray, Jr.; such organizations as the NAACP, CORE, and SNCC; and federal judges and other federal officials. In all fairness it must be admitted that Governors Hugh White (1952–1956) and James Coleman (1956–1960) were more temperate in their reactions than their successor, the extreme segregationist Barnett. But throughout the decade anyone who dared oppose the official position did so on uneven terms—and with full knowledge that to speak out could bring retaliation.

A significant part of the persuasive effort involved extrinsic controls, which are usually considered beyond the realm of traditional rhetoric. Mississippi's Establishment was formidable because it monopolized the principal means of communication. State printing contracts went to those who supported orthodoxy. State funds were actually used to produce materials for indoctrination. The leading Jackson papers, the *Daily News* and the *Clarion Ledger*, as well as the majority of rural papers, promoted the cause through slanted coverage and editorials. Editors who protested were abused, threatened, and boycotted. The *Citizen*, a little magazine first called the *Citizens' Council*, became an official organ for segregationist orthodoxy. Anonymous pamphlets and handbills and selected speeches were distributed. Whisper campaigns prevailed. School textbooks were scrutinized. In fact, "safe" books were written for the grade schools. Newspapers and magazines from outside were declared subversive and forced from the newsstands. Racist recordings produced by local groups in Jackson blared from the jukeboxes in bars and bus stations. State employees were forced to take oaths of allegiance. University professors were carefully watched, and students were encouraged to report questionable teachers. Preachers were pressured into disassociating themselves from churches that had ties or controls beyond the state borders. Ministers and professors who remained outspoken were driven from the state.[6]

6. *Ibid.*, 38–39, 60–71; John Jellicorse, Lecture at Conference on Rhetoric of the Contemporary South, Boone, North Carolina, June 28, 1974. See also eyewitness

Anyone who recommended moderation, deplored racism, suggested abiding by federal court decisions, or urged respect for federal authority could be chastised. Negroes who dared ask questions or protest or who tried to register to vote ran the risk of being beaten, burned out, or even lynched. Two Mississippi political scientists summarized the climate: "Punishment for the rebellious has often been swift and cruel. . . . Many of the more sophisticated middle class do not condone such tactics, but neither do they dare object to the activities of the rebellious."[7]

In some instances, respected citizens said nothing because they were kept ignorant of how controls were maintained. But a Millsaps College political science teacher offered other explanations. "While many people in Mississippi stand on the sidelines of 'civil rights' controversies out of fear, many more do so because they feel dwarfed by the immensity of the problems that face all of America."[8] Seeing and hearing no evil, many Mississippians wanted to believe, and in some cases actually did believe, that all was well. Inquiry about what was taking place in a given community brought assurances from opinion leaders that race relations were good and blacks were happy.

The existence of intimidation and terror as means of control was well documented in the civil rights hearings held in Jackson on February 16 through 20, 1965. Church burnings, beatings, economic reprisals, shootings, bombings, murders, cross burnings, lynchings, unlawful imprisonment, heavy fines for minor offenses, delays in processing legal documents, and harassment on streets and highways were weapons used against those who dared to oppose the

---

accounts by Mississippians: Willie Morris, *Yazoo: Integration in a Deep South Town* (New York, 1971); Oliver Emmerich, *Two Faces of Janus: The Saga of the Deep South Change* (Hattiesburg, 1973); Robert W. Canzoneri, *I Do So Politely: A Voice from the South* (Boston, 1965); Florence Mars, *Witness in Philadelphia* (Baton Rouge, 1977); P. D. East, *The Magnolia Jungle: The Life, Times, and Education of a Southern Editor* (New York, 1960); Hodding Carter, *So the Heffners Left McComb* (Garden City, N.Y., 1965).

7. Fortenberry and Abney, "Mississippi: Unreconstructed and Unredeemed," 490.

8. Gordon Henderson, "Mississippi: The Most Open Place," *New South* (October, 1965), 11.

Establishment. When abused persons asked law enforcement officers to protect them, they were ignored or in some cases subjected to further indignities. Numerous black citizens, lifetime residents of the state, testified to the prevalence of these conditions over many years, starting long before 1954, and recounted how the strategy of terror deterred them from questioning the system.

Father Luke Mikschl, who headed a school in Canton, Mississippi, spoke of "living in an atmosphere of fear." Not just Negroes, but whites also, were "afraid to come out and make themselves known." Sociologist James W. Prothro of the University of North Carolina was thwarted through "the most extreme intimidation" in doing a survey concerning civil rights among black teachers. He found that "62 percent of the teachers declined to give the interview with the explanation that the superintendent of the schools had instructed them through their principal not to discuss civil rights with anyone."[9]

At the same time that it spread fear at the grass roots, the White Citizens' Council showed the other face of Janus in public statements. Its leaders repeatedly avowed their abhorrence of lawlessness. John Bartlow Martin noted in 1957 that the council outwardly advocated only legal restraints and economic boycott to achieve its ends. To keep their reputations unsullied, the leaders sought prominent citizens as members and expounded the council's message before service clubs such as the Kiwanis, the Rotary Club, Civitan, the Exchange Club, and the Lions. They held open meetings in public buildings and insisted they were not anti-Catholic or anti-Semitic or sympathetic with the Klan.[10]

In this essay the focus is upon the official rhetoric, especially upon what prominent leaders said. Equally important, but not dealt with here, were the efforts of minor politicians, country editors, Klansmen, and John Birchers. Much of this rhetoric is not available because

9. U.S. Commission on Civil Rights, *Hearings Before the United States Commission on Civil Rights: Hearings Held in Jackson, Mississippi, February 16–20, 1965* (2 vols.; 1965), I, 207–12, II, 212.

10. John Bartlow Martin, *The Deep South Says "Never"* (New York, 1957), 30–32.

it was impromptu or extemporaneous and was intended only for friends, close associates, and neighbors.

The principal spokesmen were members of Congress, governors, and other state officials and leaders as well as officials of the White Citizens' Council. Knowing that because of their prominence, what they said would be quoted abroad and taken into account by federal judges and federal officials, these rhetoricians often attempted to demonstrate a restraint and dignity not characteristic at the grass roots. Their eagerness to drum up support outside the state is illustrated in a statement by Governor Paul B. Johnson, who said in 1964 that his primary objective was "to spearhead an all out effort to secure cooperation from other state governors and leaders to get the left-wingers out of the White House."[11] When many of the speeches are lifted out of their immediate context of tension and strife, they appear comparatively mild and general. In the heat of the moment, however, this rhetoric was the smokescreen for coercion and for the violence that erupted in many communities.

The spokesmen for the Establishment used six strategies to promote, maintain, and tighten their control. The first was to keep foremost in the minds of Mississippians the official orthodoxy of white supremacy and segregation which was "almost identical with the pro-slavery philosophy." Much like the congregation that continually needs to have the minister sanctify the articles of faith, white Mississippians yearned to hear "metaphysicians of the master racists" fortify their belief in white superiority and relieve them of guilt feelings about mistreating blacks and disobeying the laws and federal court rulings. The orators made a holy cause out of maintaining "racial integrity." Said one speaker, "There you have an issue that has just as much moral sanction . . . as much of the Holy Grail appeal as any issue on earth. You won't find a pastor in any church in America who can choose a text to surpass it."[12]

11. Paul B. Johnson, Speech to Leadership Conference of Citizens' Councils of America, quoted in *Citizen* (December, 1963), 8.

12. Silver, "Mississippi: The Closed Society," 15; Carleton Putnam, Speech at Jackson, Mississippi, in *Congressional Record*, 87th Cong., 2nd Sess., 959–63.

Judge Thomas P. Brady of Brookhaven and Carleton Putnam, a successful airline executive, became the foremost expounders of the white citizens' creed. Immediately after the decision in the case of *Brown v. The Board of Education of Topeka* in 1954, Brady answered it in a speech entitled "Black Monday," delivered at Greenwood on July 8 and Indianola on October 28. The expression used as the title referred to the day the *Brown* decision was handed down—Monday, May 17, 1954—and it was first used by Representative John Bell Williams. Later, Brady expanded the address into a ninety-page treatise that became a kind of primer of racial theories and "the first handbook for the Council movement."[13] The Mississippi legislature elevated its status by giving a commendation to Brady.

Brady delivered a bold defense of white supremacy before the Commonwealth Club of San Francisco on October 4, 1957. He called segregation "a precious and sacred custom . . . our dearest and most treasured possession" and expressed weariness over "fighting four great lies . . . [that there are] no racial differences save that of our skin, hair and eyes . . . that laws create secondclass citizenship . . . that segregation is un-Christian . . . that all men are created equal." Assuring his listeners that southerners did not hate the Negro, that Negroes and whites "lived harmoniously together with a minimum of violence and bloodshed," and that segregation did not handicap Negroes, Brady then declared that blacks were inferior, immoral, vulgar, and criminal. "[The] great gulf of difference between the I.Q. of the Negro . . . and the average white man . . . is because of deficiency in mental ability [and] . . . is due to indifference and indolence on the part of the Negroes. . . . They [white parents] are not going to permit their sons and daughters to be subjected to the vulgarity of Negro boys and girls. . . . We cannot count for naught the natural indolence and indifference of the Negro's nature. We cannot disregard his utter disregard for the laws . . . his proclivity for

13. Thomas P. Brady, *Black Monday* (Winona, Miss., 1955); Neil R. McMillen, *The Citizens' Council: Organized Resistance to the Second Reconstruction, 1954–64* (Urbana, 1971), 17–18.

drunkenness and dope addiction . . . his natural tendency to immorality and violence."[14]

Drawing upon the myths of the Old South and the Lost Cause, Brady revived southerners' horror of Reconstruction, declaring that the "Northern victor, devoid of mercy and gallantry," had illegally passed and coerced the southern states into accepting the Fourteenth Amendment. With the northern victor he associated such terms as "hatred and determination," "high-handed," "unlawful," and "corruption." Suggesting a parallel between Reconstruction and the existing situation, he recounted: "Drunken, marauding bands of crazed Negroes shot and broke into homes, raping and killing the women and children whom they dragged screaming from their flaming homes. The crackle of the flames and the groans and screams of the helpless victims, though not loud, are still audible in the mind of southerners." Judge Brady stirred enthusiasm among white southerners, many of whom quoted him frequently.

Carleton Putnam wrote a book, *Race and Reason: A Yankee View*, that was accepted as "a veritable white supremacist's catechism" or what another authority called "something of a Bible to the counter revolutionary South." In six months it sold 60,000 copies, and by 1969 some 150,000 had been distributed. Putnam received many invitations to address southern whites and was more popular in Mississippi than anywhere else.[15]

Putnam, a self-announced authority on anthropology and segregation, lent his hand to sanctifying white supremacy. Coming from a well-known outsider, his reaffirmation and elevation of the creed contributed to the continued rationalization of segregation by many southern whites. He demonstrated his rhetorical power at a

14. Thomas P. Brady, "Segregation and the South," in *Contemporary Forum: American Speeches on Twentieth Century Issues*, ed. Ernest Wrage and Barnet Baskerville (New York, 1962), 333–43.

15. Carleton Putnam, *Race and Reason: A Yankee View* (Washington, D.C., 1961); Francis M. Wilhoit, *The Politics of Massive Resistance* (New York, 1973), 96; McMillen, *The Citizens' Council*, 166.

dinner held in his honor in Jackson on October 26, 1961. Adding status to the occasion, Dr. W. D. McCain, president of Mississippi Southern College, in an extensive introduction, presented Putnam as "a businessman, flier, scholar, historian, writer, biographer, and philosopher." [16]

Putnam played up to the egotism of white Mississippians by calling them "an experienced people" who had self-discipline and were fighting for the "very integrity of civilization." He praised them for not falling "victim to the ceaseless barrage of false science, false sentimentality and false political theory." He told his listeners that they "must unmask the deception" of "politically motivated equalitarian propaganda [that] had infiltrated the life sciences since New Deal Days and had spread . . . throughout our churches and colleges." He directed the main thrust of his argument toward answering "the equalitarian findings" of anthropologist Franz Boas of Columbia University.

In rebuttal to those he called centralists, left-wingers, and pseudo-scientists who were guilty of grabbing power, "equalitarian deception," half-truths, and ignorance, Putnam cited Henry Garrett, a retired professor of psychology from Columbia, and several other persons. To strengthen his own ethos, Putnam called attention to the reception of his own *Race and Reason*, which he complained had been grossly misrepresented. [17]

The second strategy used by the spokesmen for the Establishment was to place great emphasis upon legitimatizing both the defiance of federal authority and the denial of civil rights. In 1955, Senator James O. Eastland, in the role of father figure, assured a Jackson audience that "our position is sound under the Constitution and the laws of the United States" and that the Mississippi leadership was

16. W. D. McCain, Speech introducing Carleton Putnam, in *Congressional Record*, 87th Cong., 2nd Sess., 958–60.

17. Putnam called his speech "This Is the Time." It was published in the *Congressional Record*, 87th Cong., 2nd Sess., 959–64, and in the *Citizen* (November, 1961), 12–33. He summarized this speech in *The Road to Reversal* (Richmond, n.d.).

attempting "the preservation of the American system of government with its dual powers which provide for additional liberty and freedom." He added, "The Supreme Court of the United States, in the false name of law and justice, has perpetrated a monstrous crime." Remembering the writings of John C. Calhoun, he and other leaders argued that the federal government had no right to intercede within the sovereign state of Mississippi and recommended "interposition" and defiance of federal mandates.[18]

Judge Brady declared: "The South is the citadel of conservatism. It is a fortress for constitutional government." Pursuing this line, these speakers thought that they had a redoubtable position because they stood for the preservation of freedom and justice. To give further credibility to their legitimatizing, these leaders insisted that segregation was sanctioned by Christianity and the Scriptures; or as Roy V. Harris, president of the Citizens' Councils of America, put it, separation of the races was "neither illegal, un-American nor un-Christian."[19] Furthermore, state officials assured white Mississippians that the scathing verbal attacks on the President and the justices of the Supreme Court, defiance of federal authority and the Civil Rights Commission, and local acts of harassment were not in conflict with the teachings of Christ, the Bill of Rights, the Constitution, the Declaration of Independence, or the teachings of Thomas Jefferson and other revered southerners. These appeals were indeed attractive to white Mississippians, most of whom were conservative, Protestant fundamentalists who wanted to believe they were law-abiding citizens, good Christians, and faithful adherents to "the southern way of life."

The third strategy was to maintain a positive and unyielding

18. James O. Eastland, *We've Reached Era of Judicial Tyranny* (Greenwood, Miss., n.d.). This pamphlet is the printed version of an address delivered before the State-wide Convention of Mississippi Councils at Jackson, Mississippi, on December 1, 1955.

19. Brady, "Segregation and the South," 339; Roy V. Harris, Speech to Leadership Conference of Citizens' Councils of America, quoted in *Citizen* (December, 1963), 19.

stance. Hence, the official speakers, particularly the governors, spoke in categorical absolutes. Governor Barnett told white Mississippians that "all our resources—both public and private, must be fully utilized" and "the left-wing elements . . . must be completely and utterly crushed." He also declared: "To win this life-or-death fight we must start with total mobilization of all our resources. . . . We must eliminate the cowards from our front lines." He told the voters how far he was willing to go to deter the federal government. "There is no sacrifice which I will shrink from making to preserve the social integrity of our people and institutions. Every man holding public office should feel the same way."[20]

The tone of this rhetoric is reflected in such phrases as "life-or-death fight" and "total mobilization." With their own actions the speakers associated "courage" and "strength," while those who opposed or questioned them were guilty of "cowardice," "complacency," and "failure."

In promoting this positive image, the white leaders declared that they would tolerate no compromise and that they opposed the moderates as much as they did the integrationists. In 1955 Senator Eastland warned that if Mississippi were to "knuckle under" to the threat it faced, then "every right we have is gone." He called for whites to "guard against the gradual acceptance and the erosion of our rights through the deadly doctrine of gradualism." Likewise, State Representative Brown Williams of Neshoba County, at the time a candidate for lieutenant governor, opposed compromise and said there was "no place for moderates."[21]

In 1960, after two unsuccessful campaigns for governor, Barnett projected his determination to resist at all cost any change in the racial status quo, and he won the governorship. He chastised his predeces-

---

20. Ross R. Barnett, Speech to Fund-Raising Dinner, Jackson, Mississippi, quoted in *Southern School News* (October, 1959), 3; Ross R. Barnett, Television and Radio Address, quoted in *Citizen* (September, 1962), 7.

21. Eastland, *We've Reached Era of Judicial Tyranny*, 7; Brown Williams, Speech to Leland Rotary Club, quoted in *Southern School News* (November, 1958), 4.

sors for being too mild in meeting the threat of integration and insisted he would "strongly oppose any attempt by so-called 'moderates' or 'left-wingers' to weaken in any way our traditional customs and separation of the races." In 1962 Governor Barnett declared: "The day of expediency is past. We must either submit to the unlawful dictates of the Federal Government or stand up like men and tell them 'never!'"[22]

Declaring himself "a vigorous segregationist," Barnett emphasized that he would "fight any moderate attitudes. Moderation is the foot in the door for integration." Implying guilt by association, he told a fund-raising dinner of the Jackson Citizens' Council, "These moderates . . . are nothing more than southern burglars. They want to rob us of our priceless heritage." Even after the end of his term, James Meredith's entrance into the University of Mississippi, and the advent of significant black voter registration, Barnett still maintained his rigid position. At a leadership conference of the Citizens' Council in 1965, he reasserted that he "believed in . . . never compromising with something that we know is wrong."[23] Like a fundamentalist minister, he preached that an action is either completely right or completely wrong, and this rigid either-or orientation toward the issue of integration made the justification of violence easier. His extravagant rhetoric made devil words out of "moderation," "gradualism," and "compromise."

A fourth strategy was to maintain a stout defense of the good character of Mississippians. They had a "terrible yearning for respectability," and they wanted to keep their reputations unsullied. The leaders put much stress upon the line that "the good people" did not condone violence.[24]

22. Ross R. Barnett, *Strength Through Unity* (Greenwood, Miss., n.d.); Barnett, Television and Radio Address, 7–9.

23. Ross R. Barnett, quoted in *Southern School News* (September, 1959), 5; Barnett, Speech to Fund-Raising Dinner, 3; Ross R. Barnett, Speech to Leadership Conference of Citizens' Councils of America, quoted in *Citizen* (March 1965), 17.

24. Martin, *The Deep South Says "Never,"* 15.

In 1956, in his inaugural address, Governor James P. Coleman said: "I would like you, our friends outside of Mississippi, to know that the great overwhelming majority of the white people of Mississippi are not now guilty and never intended to be guilty of any murder, violence, or other wrong doing toward anyone. . . . Despite all the propaganda which has been fired at us, the country can be assured that the white people of Mississippi are not a race of Negro killers." Likewise, Senator Eastland reminded Mississippians: "Acts of violence and lawlessness have no place. . . . In this fight no one should be mistreated. . . . The white people . . . desire peace and harmony." [25]

White Mississippians also answered the charge that they were racists. The Reverend G. T. Gillespie, retired president of Belhaven College, accomplished a neat rhetorical twist by proposing that instead of speaking of race prejudice, one should speak of "race pride," which he explained was "a rational, normal, positive principle and essentially constructive and moral." In this sentence the preacher demonstrated the rhetorical technique of substituting positive words for those with negative connotations.[26] State Senator W. B. Alexander gave the assurance that "we have nothing but friendship for good colored people." Judge Brady told the Commonwealth Club of San Francisco that "the South does not hate the Negro. . . . As a matter of fact, there is a good deal of genuine affection and understanding between the races." In his inaugural address Governor Coleman, a moderate compared to his successors, reminded the voters that "for 90 years the white and Negro people of Mississippi have lived side by side in peace and harmony." [27]

25. James P. Coleman, Inaugural Address, in *Congressional Record*, 84th Cong., 2nd Sess., appendix, A686; Eastland, *We've Reached Era of Judicial Tyranny*, 8–9.

26. G. T. Gillespie, *A Christian View on Segregation* (Jackson, 1954), printed version of a speech made before the synod of Mississippi of the Presbyterian Church, Jackson, Mississippi, November 4, 1954.

27. W. B. Alexander, Speech before Mississippi Senate, in *Congressional Record*, 84th Cong., 2nd Sess., appendix, A3364; Brady, "Segregation and the South," 335; Coleman, Inaugural Address.

When a lynching occurred at Poplarville in Pearl River County, Governor Coleman, disturbed and embarrassed, reaffirmed his earlier assertion at a news conference. "The overwhelming majority of Mississippians . . . do not approve of taking the law into their own hands." With reference to this same incident Judge Brady demonstrated he was a master rhetorician. After he declared that the Citizens' Council was "unalterably opposed to the use of violence in any form" and that its leaders believed "in working within the framework of the constitution and laws," Brady directed attention away from the lynching and stirred hatred toward the council's adversaries. "While we deplore the incident and trust the law will take its course and punish the offenders," he said, "we believe the NAACP and the other left-wing groups will rejoice in this highly regrettable incident." [28]

A fifth characteristic of the rhetoric of the Mississippi Establishment was to rationalize that outside evil forces were responsible for its plight. Mississippians argued that they were innocent victims of a plot fomented by the NAACP, the Supreme Court, the northern press, left-wing educators, left-wing pseudoscientists, professional agitators, Communists, Communist front organizations, and foundations. Senator Eastland declared: "The Supreme Court of the United States has perpetrated a monstrous crime . . . and has responded to a radical pro-Communist political movement in this country. . . . The South today is the victim of forces and influences that originated far from its own borders. . . . When groups can subvert the highest Court of the land and control the President of the United States they must be reckoned with." Dressing up the legend, John Bell Williams said that the justices "exchanged their judicial robes for the caps and gowns of sociology professors and proceeded to tear the heart from the American Constitution by their fantastic ruling in the school-segregation cases." Roy V. Harris, president of the Citizens' Councils of America, spoke of "Federal troops, the National Guard, and the

28. James P. Coleman, News Conference, quoted in *Southern School News* (May, 1959), 8; Thomas P. Brady, quoted in *Southern School News* (May, 1959), 8.

police . . . knocking white people in the head, locking them up in jails and forcing them to submit to the tyrannical orders of the Courts. . . . In order to fight this insidious movement—which originated with the Communists, the pinks and the radicals throughout the Nation—decent white people must organize and stick together." Governor Barnett told a radio and television audience, "We see our own Federal government teamed up with a motley array of un-American pressure groups against us."[29]

Noticeable in this rhetoric were such provocative words as "outside agitators," "monstrous crime," "fantastic ruling," and "naked and arbitrary orders." This intensely negative loading permitted Mississippians to absolve themselves of guilt, and it associated evil with the federal government and communism. Such language encouraged excessive reactions at the local level and doubtless contributed to the violence. In this climate the rabble-rousers indulged in wanton acts. The governor and state police did not and probably could not control the outpouring of hate once it was set in motion. Then, expressing helplessness and dismay, officials lamented that they could not prevent what the federal government had illegally started.

A sixth strategy of the Mississippi Establishment was to insist upon the necessity for unity. In the words of Barnett, Mississippians were asked to "stand together hand and hand, mind to mind" to meet the threat of sinister forces. As Governor Coleman expressed it, "Unity must be preserved at all costs and I urge the assistance and cooperation of all persons and groups to the end that we may present a united front." The officialdom and spokesmen of the White Citizens' Council stressed the need for countering the federal threats through unity. In a speech to a Citizens' Council rally in New Orleans on March 7, 1960, Governor Barnett spoke of "strength through unity" and maintained that "a united South will have a tremendous influ-

29. Eastland, *We've Reached Era of Judicial Tyranny*, 4, 6; John Bell Williams, Speech to Defenders of State Sovereignty and Individual Liberties, in *Congressional Record*, 85th Cong., 1st Sess., 4340; Harris, Speech to Leadership Conference of Citizens' Councils of America, 20, 22; Barnett, Television and Radio Address, 7.

ence." Of course, implied in the term *unity* was conformity. Paul B. Johnson, governor-elect in 1963, said, "The only way . . . to preserve our way of life is for people in every county or parish . . . to band themselves together into strong local Citizens' Councils." Senator Eastland assured Mississippians, "Right-minded people and men of goodwill from every corner of this country will join us."[30]

These pleas for unity were reminiscent of earlier appeals to the myth of the Solid South. In fact, Representative W. M. Colmer said, "We must have a new 'Solid South'—a unified, politically 'Solid South.'"[31] The effect of this rhetoric was to give the faithful the secure feeling that they were not alone and to make opposition or moderation difficult. When speakers spoke of preserving "the southern way of life," they evoked the southern mythology of the past. The net result of this strategy was to increase conformity and encourage sacrifice for the system.

With the creed of white supremacy firmly set, the state's leadership almost closed Mississippi through rigid control over communication and effective suppression of opposition. Rationalizing the sordidness of their methods, they kept attention focused upon scapegoats, including Negroes, moderates, outsiders, federal officials, and Communists. With religious fervor, they intensified emotional reactions through touting the myths of the Old South, the Lost Cause, and the Solid South.

The question arises as to whether the official rhetoric supported or sanctioned violence. Sometimes acts of violence were decried by high officials such as Governor Coleman. The spirit of such declarations is difficult to accept in light of the fact that over the decade state officials and legislators almost never took strong stands to prevent Klansmen

---

30. Coleman, Inaugural Address; Ross R. Barnett, *Strength Through Unity*; Johnson, Speech to Leadership Conference of Citizens' Councils of America, 8–11; Eastland, *We've Reached Era of Judicial Tyranny*, 15.

31. W. M. Colmer, Address to Kiwanis Club, Jackson, Mississippi, November 9, 1955, quoted in *Southern School News* (December, 1955), 11.

and hoodlums from terrorizing fellow citizens. Eyewitnesses, many of whom were victims, testified that when they were harassed, they were unable to get protection or even hearings from sheriffs, mayors, and the governor.[32] How could officials have ignored the infiltration of Klansmen into the agencies of law enforcement? Why did leaders refuse to take decisive action when citizens, white and black, were terrified and sometimes brutally murdered?

Furthermore, the direction of the official rhetoric of Mississippi remained consistent with the Klan's announced program. Although publicly state officials decried the lawlessness, the Establishment had many of the same objectives as the Klan, and at the local level the Citizens' Council, the John Birch Society, and the Klan had overlapping memberships. What were average citizens to believe when they heard governors, United States senators and representatives, and state judges advocate defiance of federal authority and refuse to consider alternate positions? Yet it seems unlikely that many leaders failed to see that their resistance was doomed or to realize that their racial rhetoric would make eventual reconciliation more painful.

The strategy and results in Mississippi were not too different from those in Germany and Italy before World War II and in other closed societies. They suggest the principle that humane government works best when the citizenry can express opposition through vigorous public debate, when there is a free flow of information, and when responsible leaders hold to the democratic ethic.

32. Carter, *So the Heffners Left McComb*, 73–128.

Selected Bibliography

For more comprehensive bibliographies on the topic of southern oratory, see my *Oratory in the Old South, 1828–1860*, and *Oratory in the New South*.

Baskerville, Barnet. *The People's Voice: The Orator in American Society*. Lexington, Ky., 1979.

Braden, Waldo W. "Southern Oratory Reconsidered: A Search for an Image." *Southern Speech Journal*, XXIX (1964), 303–15.

———, ed. *Oratory in the New South*. Baton Rouge, 1979.

———, ed. *Oratory in the Old South, 1828–1860*. Baton Rouge, 1970.

Braden, Waldo W., and Ralph T. Eubanks. "Dallas C. Dickey: Pioneer of the Critical Study of Southern Public Address." *Southern Speech Communication Journal*, XLIV (1979), 119–46.

Braden, Waldo W., and William Strickland, comps. "Southern Public Address: A Bibliography of Theses and Dissertations." *Southern Speech Communication Journal*, XLI (1976), 388–409.

Campbell, J. Louis III. "In Search of the New South." *Southern Speech Communication Journal*, XLVII (1982), 361–88.

Carleton, William G. "The Celebrity Cult a Century Ago." *Georgia Review*, XIV (1960), 133–42.

Cash, W. J. *The Mind of the South*. New York, 1941.

Cooper, William J., Jr. *The South and the Politics of Slavery 1828–1856*. Baton Rouge, 1978.

Degler, Carl N. *Place over Time: The Continuity of Southern Distinctiveness*. Baton Rouge, 1977.

Dickey, Dallas C. "Were They Ephemeral and Florid?" *Quarterly Journal of Speech*, XXXII (1946), 16–20.

Dorgan, Howard. "A Case Study in Reconciliation: General John B. Gordon and 'The Last Days of the Confederacy.'" *Quarterly Journal of Speech*, LX (1974), 83–91.

————. "The Doctrine of Victorious Defeat in Rhetoric of Confederate Veterans." *Southern Speech Communication Journal*, XXXVIII (1972), 119–30.

Gaines, Francis Pendleton. *Southern Oratory: A Study in Idealism*. University, Ala., 1946.

Gaston, Paul M. *The New South Creed: A Study in Southern Mythmaking*. New York, 1970.

Green, Fletcher M. "Listen to the Eagle Scream: One Hundred Years of the Fourth of July in North Carolina (1776–1876)." *North Carolina Historical Review*, XXXI (1954), 295–320, 529–49.

Logue, Cal M., and Howard Dorgan, eds. *The Oratory of the Southern Demagogues*. Baton Rouge, 1981.

Saxon, John D. "Contemporary Southern Oratory: A Rhetoric of Hope, not Desperation." *Southern Speech Communication Journal*, XLI (1975), 262–74.

Weaver, Richard M. *The Southern Tradition at Bay: A History of Postbellum Thought*. New Rochelle, N.Y., 1968.

Index